BARRON'S BUSINESS KEYS

KEYS TO MORTGAGE FINANCING AND REFINANCING

Fourth Edition

Jack P. Friedman, PhD, CPA, MAI, CRE
Real Estate Consultant and Appraiser
Dallas, Texas

Jack C. Harris, PhD
Real Estate and Mortgage Consultant
Crystal Beach, Florida

BARRON'S

All inquiries should be addressed to:
Barron's Educational Series, Inc.
250 Wireless Boulevard
Hauppauge, NY 11788
http://www.barronseduc.com

Library of Congress Catalog Card Number 2006021679

ISBN-13: 978-0-7641-3531-6
ISBN-10: 0-7641-3531-7

Library of Congress Cataloging-in-Publication Data
Friedman, Jack P.
    Keys to mortgage financing and refinancing / Jack P. Friedman, Jack C. Harris. — 4th ed.
        p. cm. — (Barron's business keys)
    Includes index.
    ISBN-13: 978-0-7641-3531-6
    ISBN-10: 0-7641-3531-7
    1. Mortgage loans. 2. Mortgage loans—Refinancing. 3. Home equity loans. I. Harris, Jack C., 1945- II. Title.

HG2040.15.F74 2006
332.7′22—dc22   2006021679

Printed in the United States of America
9 8 7 6 5 4 3 2 1

CONTENTS

1

MORTGAGE LOAN OVERVIEW

The vast majority of homes are purchased with mortgage loans. When you borrow money on a home, you are committing yourself to two financial documents. The *note* is a personal obligation to repay the loan on a timely basis. The *mortgage* pledges the home as security in case you fail to live up to your obligation. You, as the borrower, give a mortgage to the lender to secure the loan. Therefore, you are referred to as the *mortgagor*, and the lender is the *mortgagee*—the receiver of the mortgage. This document sets out the obligations you are expected to meet and defines your rights and those of the lender.

All mortgage loans have an interest rate and a term. The interest rate is applied to the amount of money you borrowed and haven't yet paid back. You pay this interest in monthly installments. In addition to interest, your payment includes an extra amount to pay back the principal. Therefore, the principal balance is reduced with each payment. This means that the interest payment is also reduced, as time passes.

Since the total payment remains constant, more money is applied to principal reduction as the loan ages. The payment schedule is designed so that the loan will be completely paid off at the end of the term even though few mortgage loans survive their full term. Most are ended when the home is sold or refinanced several years after the loan was originated.

Definitions of a few key terms are provided below to help you better understand mortgage financing. (A more extensive glossary begins on page 163.)

Amortization is the process of paying down the principal of the loan. If the interest rate on the loan is fixed, an amortization schedule for the full term can be prepared when the loan is originated.

Fixed-rate loans have the same interest rate applied over the entire term. The combined monthly payment for principal and interest is unchanged.

Adjustable-rate mortgages (ARMS) provide for adjustments to the interest rate at specified intervals. When the rate is adjusted, the principal and interest payment may change.

A *balloon payment* occurs when the term of the loan is shorter than the full amortization term. Most balloon payment loans are made by nonprofessional lenders, such as sellers who provide financing to induce a sale. They want to limit the life of the loan without making monthly payments prohibitively high. When a balloon payment becomes due, the borrower will have to refinance the loan.

Refinancing is the process of replacing the current financing with a new loan or set of loans. This may involve replacing the original loan with one of the same amount, increasing the amount of the loan, or replacing several mortgages with one mortgage loan.

Loan assumption is the process of allowing a later home buyer to take over the existing loan, possibly substituting for the seller. Many loans have due-on-sale provisions that prevent assumptions. Loans that don't are called *assumable mortgages.*

An *escrow account is* required by most lenders. The account provides funds to pay for hazard insurance and property taxes. The borrower makes a deposit in the account with each monthly payment (the total payment is sometimes called PITI, for principal, interest, taxes, and insurance). Since insurance premiums and taxes may vary, the monthly payment may change over time even for fixed-rated loans.

A *loan commitment* indicates the lender's intention to provide a loan with specified terms. The lender has to process the loan application before the loan is approved, but a rate commitment may be granted when you apply. This states that if the loan is approved, it will be for a certain amount and have certain terms.

A loan closing, also called *settlement,* marks the time when the money is provided (usually coinciding with the closing of the sale) and interest starts to accrue. Payments are often timed to be paid at the beginning of the month and include interest that has accrued during the previous month. Interest accruing between the closing and the end of the month is paid at the closing.

The mortgage market offers several variations on the traditional fixed-interest-rate, level-payment mortgage loan. Some loans do not require a payment toward principal reduction; some even allow you to defer payment of some of the interest owed. In all of these loan types, interest is accrued on the full amount of the outstanding principal, but it is paid back in various ways. Some loans allow the lender to change the interest rate at pre-established intervals. Such loans shift some of the financial risks inherent in the loan onto the borrower. In other words, if interest rates rise over the term of the loan, the borrower will face higher monthly payments (of course, payments would decline if rates fall). Borrowers usually require a lower initial interest rate to take on this additional risk. A good understanding of how mortgage loans work (which is the object of this book) will allow you to better shop and negotiate the loan market.

2

HOME FINANCING IN THE TWENTY-FIRST CENTURY

The early years of the twenty-first century have produced one of the most vigorous and durable housing booms in modern history. The percentage of households in the United States that own the home they live in advanced from 66.7 in 1999 to over 69 by late 2004 and has never been higher. Existing home sales were up 30% and new home sales were up 36% over that time. Real estate has become the preferred investment medium for many. Remarkably, this boom has occurred while the economy has struggled to expand and without high rates of inflation, two factors formerly considered the prerequisites to a real estate boom.

One of the driving forces behind the surge in housing demand is the decline in mortgage interest rates beginning in the 1990s and continuing into the 2000s. Mortgage rates have remained historically low even in the face of a series of interest rate hikes by the Federal Reserve Bank. Low interest rates mean that borrowers need less income to qualify for a loan of a given amount. Accordingly, the same income allows a borrower to buy a more expensive home, and home prices have risen as a consequence. Strangely enough, rising prices also stimulate demand because they make houses appear to be better investments (buyers tend to believe that recent price increases portend further increases in the future).

Not only have interest rates declined, but mortgage loans have become easier to obtain. People who, in the past, were shunned by the mortgage market have become target markets for new loans. There are special mort-

4

gages aimed at those who have never owned a home, for ethnic minorities, for those with no or checkered credit histories, and self-employed people who have difficulty documenting a steady income. Not only are more people aspiring to homeownership, but a broader array of people now have the financial ability to do so.

Improved access to mortgage loans is the result of major changes in the mortgage market that began in the late 1990s and came to fruition during the early 2000s. The most important of these changes are:

Where you go to get a mortgage loan: During much of the last century, most people went to specialized mortgage lending institutions, such as savings and loan associations (a.k.a. thrift institutions), when they needed to buy a home. The government tried to nurture these institutions by protecting them from competition and giving them special advantages in how they raised money and how their income was taxed. This system broke down in the 1980s when wide swings in market interest rates and high loan failure rates doomed many thrifts.

The way these lenders operated was to take in deposits from individual savers and use them to make loans. During the 1980s, a national market for loans developed and the mortgage banker—who originates and then sells the loans to investors—became the primary source of home financing. Then in the 1990s, mortgage brokers—agents who originate loans for a number of lenders—became popular because they could often find the lowest-priced financing available.

Today, being able to gather information on a number of lenders and loan products and choose from among them is well-established in the market place. The Internet allows individuals to compare the terms of a broad array of loans. For those who need more guidance, there are real and virtual mortgage brokers and bankers to help explain the options.

The move toward "one-stop shopping" is well under way. This concept allows a homebuyer to obtain financing and other purchase necessities in one convenient location. Many real estate brokerages have in-house mortgage operations to work with borrowers. In some cases, real estate agents can also help you select and apply for a loan without ever visiting a lender's office.

At the time this book was published, commercial banks were fighting to gain the right to open real estate brokerage offices. If successful, these institutions could be a major force in consolidating mortgage financing with the house purchase transaction. Another trend that could combine many functions under one roof and simplify the homebuying process is the packaging of all the services required to close a sale (title insurance, financing, hazard insurance) into one contract with a guaranteed price. Technology and competition promise to further change the way real estate is purchased.

What kind of loans you can get: In the 1980s, many different types of mortgage loans appeared, largely to cope with a high-inflation interest rate market. But these loans were basically created for the same type of borrower: those with good, established credit and enough cash to make a decent down payment. Today, almost anyone can buy a home thanks to a proliferation of loans designed for different kinds of borrowers. With very good credit, you may be able to borrow 100% of the purchase price. If you have poor credit, it is likely you can still secure a loan, albeit at a higher rate of interest. If you never bought a home before and do not have a credit record, there are a host of loans aimed at first-time homebuyers. Most of these loans feature low down payments and relaxed underwriting standards. For example, borrowers may get credit for a history of paying their rent on time.

How your loan is processed: In the past, waiting for loan approval was a long and nerve-racking experience for most homebuyers. In recent years, much of the loan underwriting process—the procedure used to decide whether the loan should be made—has been streamlined, thanks to the greater ease with which information can be accessed and transferred. Many loans are approved using computer programs that can evaluate a good deal of information pertinent to the loan. Often, the result of the process is to compute a "credit score" that determines not only whether you receive the loan, but what type of loan it is and its terms. This means that loans can be approved faster, with less hassle to the applicant. Also, fewer loans are rejected since the use of credit scores relieves the strict "go/no-go" decision.

The modern mortgage market appears to develop new products wherever there is sufficient demand. When many homeowners refinanced their mortgages as interest rates were falling, lenders began offering loans with no discount points. These loans were very popular because they reduced the cost of refinancing. Now, no-point mortgages dominate the market for purchases as well as refinancings. For self-employed borrowers and others who have trouble providing the kind of information required for loan approval, or for those who need to obtain approved financing quickly, there are loans that require little or no documentation. There are also loans for borrowers who make low down payments, but who want to avoid the requisite mortgage insurance.

Just because it is easy to get a particular loan, that does not mean that you should accept the offer. The variety of loans available includes some that are clearly not appropriate for your situation. Only by knowing how mortgage loans work and the way they can be tailored to different situations can you be sure to choose the financing that works best for you.

3

WHAT MAKES INTEREST RATES GO UP AND DOWN?

Interest is similar to rent charged for the use of other people's money. Like any other price, interest rates go up and down in response to the supply of and demand for money. The supply comes from people who invest in bonds and deposit money in bank accounts. Demand comes from many sectors, including homebuyers, consumers using credit cards, government, and business.

When money is in short supply, interest rates go up. During these periods, there is a high demand for money: people and businesses have the confidence and ability to take out loans. At times, the demand for money weakens and supply increases, so that interest rates fall. Rates also respond to public perception of risk. If the chance that a loan will be repaid becomes poor, lenders will demand a higher interest rate to compensate. If it looks like inflation will rear its ugly head, lenders demand higher interest rates to make up for the deterioration in the purchasing power of the dollars they expect to receive in the future.

There are several major factors that cause shifts in supply and demand, including:

- **Government Borrowing.** When the federal government runs a budget deficit, which it does with regularity, it must issue bonds to fund its operations, thus using up a portion of the money available to all borrowers (though some creditors would lend only to the government, considered to be a "risk-free" investment).

- **Private Debt.** When households run up debt, it also adds to the demand for money and puts upward pressure on interest rates. Households are also the source of money supplied to the markets. The extent to which a household is a net debtor or creditor is largely a function of age; however, a strong housing market can also push the balance toward the debtor side because of the heavy demand for mortgage loans.
- **Foreign Investors.** Individuals, businesses, and governments in foreign countries are of growing importance to the supply of money and capital. Foreigners are attracted to U.S. debt securities because of the relative certainty that the money will be repaid and the fact that so much U.S. currency goes to foreign countries because of our trade deficit.

Despite the influence of these factors, the most influential is the activity of the Federal Reserve Bank. The Fed is empowered to conduct monetary policy for the federal government. Essentially, that means the Fed controls a core element of the supply of currency in our economy. The Fed's primary goal is to protect the integrity of the currency, so that a dollar is worth nearly the same over time. A secondary goal is to counter the adverse effects of economic cycles and keep the economy close to full employment. The Fed tries to alter the growth of the money supply to match the demand for currency. When it is successful, inflation is low and interest rates are stable.

Economists watch an indicator called the *federal funds rate* to monitor the activity of the Fed. When the Fed thinks inflation is rising, it will try to slow the growth of the money supply by raising the federal funds rate. This is called "tightening" and leads to higher interest rates throughout the market. When the Fed thinks inflation is not a problem, but the economy is weak, it may lower the federal funds rate—"easing" monetary policy—to increase the supply of money. Interest rates fall during these periods and that tends to stimulate economic activity.

The chart shows how inflation (annual change in the consumer price index) corresponds to the federal funds rate. You can see how the Fed responded to flare ups in inflation by boosting the interest rate (the exception was a tightening in 1994 that did not respond to a rise in inflation).

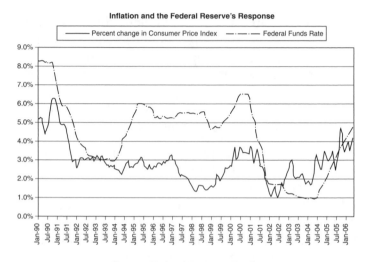

Source: Federal Reserve Bank

The Fed's actions affect mortgage interest rates significantly. A higher federal funds rate makes all money more expensive. The most sensitive rates are those for short-term obligations—consumer loans, adjustable-rate mortgages—but long-term obligations like fixed-rate mortgages are also affected. To some extent, if the market senses that the Fed is countering inflation effectively, the inflation premium portion of the interest rate will decline. For the most part, however, Fed tightening will raise mortgage rates. The sensitivity of mortgage rates to Fed actions is shown in the chart below.

Mortgage Rates and Monetary Policy

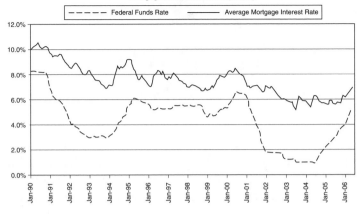

Source: Federal Reserve Bank

Note how mortgage rates tend to follow the federal funds rate. The exception here is during the period 2004–2005, when strong Fed tightening failed to have much effect on mortgages. It is thought that strong buying of U.S. debt by foreign investors largely countered the Fed's influence in this period. This lack of a simple explanation for interest rate fluctuations illustrates how difficult the task of forecasting interest rates is. In most cases, trying to time the market by guessing where interest rates will go, as when deciding when to refinance a loan, is a futile and possibly hazardous endeavor.

4

LOAN-TO-VALUE RATIO

The loan-to-value ratio is an important feature of mortgage loans. The ratio is calculated by dividing the amount of principal outstanding on the mortgage loan by the current value of the property mortgaged. It is a key piece of information anytime you are making financing decisions.

When you finance the purchase of the property, the loan-to-value ratio for available financing indicates how much cash you must raise to complete the purchase. For example, if the property costs $200,000 and loans are available at a loan-to-value ratio of 80%, you must raise $40,000 to make the down payment. The down payment may come from personal savings, proceeds from the sale of another property, loans from friends or relatives, or a second mortgage loan.

Lenders and brokers will talk of loan terms based on the loan-to-value ratio. They'll say a 90% loan is 6% interest plus 2 points; a 95% loan is 6 plus 2½. You'll catch on to this talk right away.

Once you have financed and purchased the property, the loan-to-value ratio tells you how much equity you have in the property. Your equity is the amount of property value you would have left over after you sold the property and paid back the loan. So, by knowing how much equity you have, you can estimate how much of the sale proceeds could be applied to purchasing another home. Equity also indicates how much you could raise by refinancing the property. You probably would not be able to take all of your equity out with a loan, since the lender wants to see some equity remain in the property. For example, if your home is worth $200,000 and you owe $120,000, you could raise $40,000 (less refinancing costs) by refinancing with a new loan at 80% loan-to-value.

Lenders use the loan-to-value ratio to indicate the risk of lending a mortgage loan. The higher the loan-to-value, the riskier the loan. This is because less equity means the borrower is less financially committed to the property and is more likely to default on the loan. In addition, a high loan-to-value ratio means the property is less likely to cover the loan amount if the lender has to foreclose and sell the property.

The standard home mortgage loan is for 80% of property value. Lenders will make loans for higher ratios if they are insured or guaranteed. The Federal Housing Administration (FHA) and various private companies provide insurance for such loans, and the Veterans Administration (VA) guarantees loans for qualified veterans. Mortgage insurance requires a premium to be paid by the borrower. In addition, high loan-to-value ratio loans may carry higher rates of interest than standard loans.

5

LEVERAGE

Anytime you use borrowed money to make an investment, you are using *leverage.* In the case of buying a home, you probably have little choice other than to get a mortgage loan. Very few can afford to buy a home with all cash. However, even if you did have that much cash, you might still want to borrow money to cover part of the purchase.

For one thing, you might not want to tie up a large part of your cash in property. By borrowing, you can keep those funds available for emergencies or to take advantage of good investments as they appear. You are better able to spread your funds among many investments, so that you are not so dependent on the success of each one.

Finally, using leverage can improve the performance of your investment. You may not think of buying a home as an investment, but it is. First, you are investing in housing for the future. Instead of renting a home, you are renting the money to buy that home. It is true that you could lose that home if you don't keep up the "rent" payments on the loan, but you don't have to worry about losing your lease because the owner of the property changes plans.

Furthermore, your home can return a profit if it increases in value while you own it. Leverage will increase the rate of return you may realize on appreciation. For example, if you buy a home for $200,000 cash and sell it the next year for $220,000, your rate of return would be 10% on your investment. However, if you borrowed $160,000 to buy the home, the rate of return on your $40,000 down payment would be 50%.

Refinancing to take out equity keeps the maximum leverage working for you. In the example above, say you sold the home at the end of the second year for

$240,000. With the original $160,000 loan, the return on your equity in the second year would be 33%. If you refinanced the loan after the first year for $180,000 (taking out $20,000 in cash), your return on equity in year two would be 50%.

The other side of leverage is that it increases your risk of loss. The more you borrow, the more pressure there is on your income to cover the payments on the loan. If you run into problems, you may have trouble making your payments. Also, if the property declines in value and you must sell, leverage acts to increase your loss. For example, if the $200,000 home is sold after a year for $180,000, you would suffer a loss of 10% of your investment. If you had used a loan of $160,000, however, you would have lost half of your equity.

Institutional factors also may influence the decision on how much debt to use. Interest paid on a mortgage loan is, for the most part, deductible against income taxes. This benefit reduces the ultimate cost of mortgage debt and makes it preferable to other kinds of debt that are not deductible. By increasing your amount of itemized deductions through a larger mortgage loan, you may be able to take advantage of other deductible expenses you have. These deductions are not useful unless you have enough deductible expenses to exceed the standard deduction available to taxpayers who do not itemize.

Higher mortgage debt may cost you money. The lender may charge you a higher rate of interest for a loan that bears a higher loan-to-value ratio. This is particularly problematic if your loan exceeds the limits for loans purchased by Fannie Mae and Freddie Mac. The limit for a one unit property in 2006 is $417,000. (Fannie Mae and Freddie Mac are called "Fannie" and "Freddie.") "Jumbo" mortgages carry higher interest rates. Private mortgage insurance premiums also tend to go up as the loan-to-value ratio increases.

In any financing or refinancing decision, you should keep in mind the effect the arrangement will have on your exposure to financial trouble.

6

TAX CONSIDERATIONS

The interest you pay on a mortgage loan can, in most cases, be deducted from your income for tax purposes. This deduction provided by the tax law is a key to reducing the cost of owning a home.

To use the deduction, the home must be your principal residence or a second home you use at least part of the year (rental properties have their own special rules). If the loan is the original one you used to buy the home, or was used to improve or construct it, you can deduct all interest paid on up to $1 million of the loan balance. If you have refinanced the loan or added a second mortgage since purchase, you can deduct interest paid on any loan balance up to $100,000 (over the balance on the original loan).

For example, suppose you buy a home with a loan of $280,000. Five years later, you refinance the mortgage with a new loan of $400,000. The balance on the old loan was $275,000. You can deduct interest on $275,000 of the new loan, plus another $100,000 of the new loan, for a total of $375,000. The amount of interest you paid on the remaining $25,000 of the loan is considered personal interest, which is not deductible. However, if $25,000 or more had been spent to improve the home, such as to add a room, then all of the interest would be deductible as housing interest.

Another example shows how much you can save from the tax deduction. If you get a mortgage loan for $100,000 at 7% interest for 30 years, your monthly payment is $665.30. Over the first year, you will pay $7,983.60, of which $6,967.80 is interest. By deducting this interest on your tax return, you will save $1,950.98 in taxes (at a tax rate of 28%). This means that the real cost of your mortgage payments is only $502.72 per month.

Keep in mind that if you don't itemize your deductions, you can take the standard deduction of $10,300 for a married couple in 2006. Therefore, only the amount of itemized deductions above the standard deduction actually represents tax savings. In the example above, if you had no other itemized deductions, you would be better off taking the standard deduction, and the deductibility of interest would be of no practical benefit. Note that itemized deduction amounts begin to phase out (diminish) when income exceeds around $150,000 for married taxpayers filing a joint return in 2006 (half that for singles). The exact income limit is indexed and increases each year. Consequently, for very high-income homeowners, there is no tax benefit derived from financing a home.

In some cases, you can deduct discount points paid to obtain a mortgage loan to buy a house, but not for refinancing. The points must be customarily charged in your area. If you write a separate check for these points, rather than let the lender deduct the amount from the loan, these points are tax deductible in the year they are paid. However, if the loan was used to refinance an existing loan rather than for a new purchase, you cannot deduct discount points in one year. You must spread the cost of the points over the life of the loan.

7

LOAN SHOPPING

If you've been waiting to see when interest rates will bottom out before buying, you know how difficult that can be. When rates are falling, there's a temptation to wait for a further decline before buying. But then rates can turn up sharply, and the opportunity may slip away. On the other hand, if you buy—and afterward interest rates drop even further—you may have an opportunity to refinance. Refinancing is replacing your old mortgage with a new one.

Whether it is the original mortgage or a refinancing, shop carefully for the best mortgage. A real estate broker can be helpful, but plan to spend several hours on the phone asking for rates. Some newspapers print mortgage rates offered by local lenders once a week. That, too, is useful information, but be sure to call and verify. Take out the Yellow Pages and call every lender. Ask for rates, points, and all other costs for the type of loan (e.g., FHA, fixed-rate, ARM) and repayment schedule that you want. Make a chart on which you enter each lender's name, phone number, loan officer, rate, points, fees, lock-in period, and application fees. Often, local newspapers compile a similar table and print it weekly in their business or real estate section. These tables may have week-old information, so they should be used as a guide and not as a complete substitute for the one you compile yourself. The mortgage business today is as much national as local, so you may want to include some large loan companies in your matrix. Finding information about loan terms is relatively easy over the Internet. A search of Web addresses under the topic of "mortgage loans" will give you a large cross-section of lenders from which to choose. There are Web sites that allow you to find the best rates available in your area. Among these, you might check out such sites as *http://mortgages.interest.com*, *www.hsh.com*, and *www.bankrate.com*. Regardless of whether you want to use the lenders who sponsor these sites, they provide a good benchmark for the going market rate on various types of loans in your locality.

You might also ask friends about their experiences with their lenders. Many times, it is better to deal with a lending institution that has an outstanding reputation than to attempt to get the best terms. If you are working with a real estate agent, do not hesitate to ask for a referral. Agents work closely with lenders and they know which ones are the best for completing a sale. Recognize that federal law discourages an agent from referring you to a lender because that lender offers to pay the agent a fee. However, agents may refer you to a lender with ties to the brokerage firm, or the agent may have access to a computerized network that can process loans. There are disclosures required to alert you to these arrangements, so you probably do not have to worry about being taken advantage of in such cases. On the other hand, you should have a general idea of what kind of terms are available in the market before you select a loan through these types of referrals.

Rates have a way of changing quickly, so ask about the length of the lock-in (the period for which their rate quote will be valid) and the amount of the application fee. Some lenders will offer a 60-day lock-in, but may want a 1% nonrefundable fee. Others will refuse to lock in, especially when rates are volatile, giving you the prevailing rate at closing. Beware of the lender with the lowest quote and a long lock-in.

Types of Lending Institutions. Most mortgage lenders, such as banks, sell off their loans to investors after the closing; often, even the right to service the loan (collect payments for a fee) is sold. Consequently, the identity of the original lender often doesn't matter to the borrower, who may begin dealing with someone else even before making the first payment. (Keys 8 and 10 offer descriptions of mortgage lenders.)

Guidelines of income required for various types of loans are described in Key 20. Some lenders will pre-qualify you, that is, tell you how large an amount you can borrow. When shopping for a house, this can give you confidence that you will be able to close, and will also expedite the closing time. However, most lenders won't take you seriously until you show them a signed contract to buy a house.

When you approach a lender, have all of your financial papers in order. Make a list of your accounts: checking, savings, and debts. Include account numbers and balances. Bring copies of car titles. Bring a list of securities you own and their value. Bring copies of 1099 tax forms to show dividend, interest, and royalty income. If you own rental property, bring something to prove you receive rental income. If either spouse is divorced, show proof of alimony and/or child support, whether paying or receiving. List your jobs for the past ten years, with addresses, phone numbers, income, and supervisors. Bring W-2 forms for the past two years and your Form 1040.

Your lender will want a copy of the sales contract (not necessary for a refinancing) plus details of all the other items noted above. Help the lender to verify, as this will expedite the loan process. The lender will want money for a property appraisal (about $400) and credit check ($50). Ask your lender how long the process normally takes. Call back regularly to be certain there are no unusual snags. Your seller and broker will also appreciate being kept informed of your loan approval status.

8

LOAN SOURCES: FIRST LIEN LOANS

A first lien loan is the mortgage placed on the home before any other loans are taken out. It is usually the loan you use to buy the home and may be the largest loan on the home. The lender of a first lien loan has first claim on the home in the case of default.

There are several types of lenders who specialize in making loans on homes.

S&Ls and MSBS. These are *savings and loan associations and mutual savings banks*—depository institutions that offer checking and savings accounts and use the money to make loans. Most of these institutions also operate mortgage banking operations, which makes available to them a wider variety of loans they can keep or sell. Because of certain regulations, most of the loans they make are home mortgages. The institution you deal with will probably be a local association or branch, but in some cases out-of-town lenders will be actively making loans in your area.

Mortgage Bankers. These companies make loans and sell them to investors. Incidentally, it makes little difference who owns your loan. It does make a difference who services your loan, that is, who collects the payments and handles the escrow account. In many cases, the lender who originated the loan will service it. However, it is becoming more common for the servicing to be transferred, even for loans made by local institutions. Servicing entails collecting your payments and making sure that sufficient insurance is maintained and property taxes paid.

Mortgage Brokers. These firms operate much like mortgage bankers. However, they do not use their own money to originate loans. Instead, they find the type of loan you want and originate the loan for the lender chosen. A broker may represent a number of lenders. Brokers can help you choose from among an array of loan types. Often, they can find loans that cater to special problems, such as a borrower without an established credit record. Brokers operate on fees that lenders pay for submitted loan applications.

Within limits, real estate brokers can act as mortgage brokers. Some are hooked up to special networks of mortgage lenders. Through the use of specialized computer software, the broker can access information on loans currently offered by lenders in the network and help the homebuyers select a loan and prepare a loan application, all within the real estate broker's office. If you like the convenience of such one-stop shopping, ask about the availability of "Computerized Loan Origination" when meeting with your real estate sales agent.

Other types of lenders may make home mortgage loans as well:

Commercial Banks. Although banks specialize in short-term and business loans, they are becoming more active in home mortgages, particularly adjustable-rate loans. Physically, banks and savings and loans are similar. Banks generally have the word "bank" in their title, while S&Ls often use the word "savings." If either uses the word *national* or *federal* in its title, it is chartered by the Federal Reserve System (for banks) or the Federal Home Loan Bank Board (for savings and loans or mutual banks). Others are chartered by a state authority. The difference may affect the types of loans they are allowed to offer.

Credit Unions. If you are a member of a credit union, you may be able to get a mortgage loan from this source. Credit unions specialize in smaller, short-term loans but may offer some types of home loans.

Stockbrokers. If you have an account with a stock brokerage firm, you may be able to secure a mortgage there. Most stockbrokers, even discount brokers, offer mortgage loans. If your portfolio is substantial, you may receive favorable terms on the loan. Many brokerage houses offer a "pledged asset' mortgage that obviates the need for a big cash down payment. If you pledge the portfolio as collateral on the loan, you may borrow up to 100 percent of the value of the home. Of course, you cannot liquidate the portfolio while it is pledged and you may have to add securities or money if the stocks fall in value.

Sellers. When buying a home, it is also possible to obtain financing from the seller, especially one who is anxious to move. The mortgage rate that buyer and seller agree upon may represent a happy compromise between what the seller could earn on money in the bank and what the buyer would have to pay for borrowed funds.

Refinancing Options. If you are refinancing a first mortgage, you may want to check with the original lender first. It may be possible to avoid some of the closing costs, especially if the loan was made within the past few years. You have established a payment record with the lender, so a new credit report shouldn't be needed. Also, it may be possible to use the original survey. If your lender refuses to waive these costs, you may want to consider other lenders.

9

PRE-QUALIFICATION AND PRE-APPROVAL

Many people do not think about mortgage financing until they enter into a contract to buy a home. In fact, most mortgage lenders will require you to have a signed purchase contract before you can apply for a loan. However, that does not preclude a bit of pre-arrangement on your part at the start of the home shopping process. In fact, it can save valuable time and may give you some negotiating advantage.

This financial pre-planning can take several forms, from basic research to actually starting the loan application process. The most casual effort would be to check current interest rates available from lenders in your area. This task is often simplified by the local newspapers, which commonly compile tables of current mortgage terms and report them weekly in the business, real estate, or "homes" section of the paper. Also, most real estate agents will have a list of current loan terms prepared for your perusal. If you want more information, you can call the lenders on the list. They should be willing to quote interest rates, origination fees and points, application fees, and what types of loans they offer over the phone.

The next level of preparation is to get "pre-qualified." Pre-qualification is an informal and highly simplified version of the qualification process you go through after you apply for a loan. Basically, the loan officer will apply the standard qualifying ratios to your income and debt level and determine how much loan you would qualify for if you were applying for a loan. Pre-qualification assumes that all the other things that go into the loan approval decision are acceptable. It does not indicate that you have any leg up in the loan application process. In fact, your real estate agent can probably pre-qualify you.

The purpose of pre-qualification is to get an idea of how much house you can afford. If you know how large a loan you can qualify for and how much cash you can invest, you can add the two totals to determine the most expensive house you may consider. This information can be valuable as you search the market (unless you are looking for a dream home that will likely remain a dream).

Pre-approval is more serious. With pre-approval, the lender goes through the entire loan approval process as if you were applying for the largest loan you can get. The purpose is to set a limit on your house search (as in pre-qualification) and show you are creditworthy at that level. The process must be performed by a lender (or someone authorized by the lender to process loan applications) and will probably require some type of fee (to compensate for the cost of a credit report and processing time). More importantly, you will need to decide on the lender and type of loan you plan to use to finance your eventual purchase. This is because pre-approval applies only to a specific loan offered by a specific lender. If you choose another lender or loan later on, your pre-approval will not apply.

While pre-approval shortens the loan processing time once the loan application is submitted, the real value is in the negotiating power it can provide in competitive markets. A home seller might favor a buyer with a definite chance of getting funding, this can translate into a better price or other concessions. It could prove decisive if you are a first-time buyer or if you need to make a minimal down payment.

If you have any question on how far your income will go in the current housing market, you should get pre-qualified. There is no need to waste time on homes you cannot afford. If you have any doubts about your ability to get a loan (perhaps you have had some credit problems in your past), you might find it worthwhile to get pre-approved. Or you may want to defer that decision until you test out the market and can better judge whether pre-approval will be useful.

10

LOAN SOURCES: JUNIOR LIEN LOANS

Most lenders who make first lien mortgages also provide second mortgages. These include savings and loan associations, mortgage bankers, and commercial banks. In fact, you may want to make your first inquiry for a second mortgage loan at the lender that holds your first mortgage, especially if the relationship has been good.

Because second mortgages are usually smaller and have a shorter term than first mortgages, there is a greater range of lenders involved. Traditionally, consumer finance companies have done most of the second mortgage lending when the purpose of the loan is to raise cash. These firms advertise in the newspaper and can be found in the classified section of the phone book under "Loans." Many of these companies are independent and locally owned, but some are affiliated with major national corporations.

With the advent of the home equity loan, commercial banks have aggressively marketed second mortgages. Terms may be very attractive, as the bank is interested in bringing in new customers for other services, such as checking accounts and credit cards.

In some cases, you may arrange with relatives or friends to obtain a second mortgage loan. This is for special situations, such as help in making a down payment on the home or getting through a temporary financial difficulty.

Companies that make home improvements may also provide financing for the services. They generally sell the loans to a bank or finance company for cash, which they need to stay in business. You would probably be better off approaching a lender yourself, unless you don't have the time or inclination to do so.

When shopping for a second mortgage loan, look at the terms offered on first mortgage loans. In addition, you may wish to try to minimize the costs of opening the loan, particularly if the loan amount is relatively small. A second loan involves many of the same underwriting procedures applied to first loans. This may include an appraisal of the home, a survey, and a credit check. Some lenders will waive fees or charge nominal fees for origination.

You may be able to arrange a second mortgage loan as part of a package that also includes a first mortgage. These so-called "piggyback loans" have the advantage of avoiding the mortgage insurance that would have to be carried on a first loan for more than 80 percent of value. See Key 15, "Canceling or Avoiding Private Mortgage Insurance," for more detail.

11

SPECIAL LOANS FOR FIRST-TIME HOMEBUYERS

When you buy that first home, the financial hurdles can be formidable. You need enough income to qualify for a loan sufficient to buy the home. This means you need a steady income and established credit. You need cash for a down payment, as well as for the expenses normally incurred at closing. The down payment, pre-paid expenses, and closing costs generally represent at least 5–6 percent of the cost of the home.

It is no wonder that first-time homebuyers are at a financial disadvantage. Fortunately, the government and large financial institutions recognize how important it is to maintain a steady stream of new homebuyers in the market, and they have devised a number of loan products specially tailored for first-time buyers.

Traditionally, first-time buyers turned to the FHA for help in getting a loan. Loan insurance from FHA, the 203(b) program, allows borrowers to buy with a down payment of as little as 3 percent of the cost of the home. The program is not restricted to first-time homebuyers, but statutory restrictions on the size of loans that can be insured tend to target the program toward those buying their first home.

The big secondary purchasers of mortgage loans (that is, buyers of existing first mortgages), Fannie Mae and Freddie Mac, each offer programs intended to help first-time buyers. Like FHA, they are not restricted to first-time buyers, but they contain features that are especially helpful to first-timers. The loans have names like

"Affordable Gold" or "Fannie 97." The essential features of these loans include:

- A low down payment with provisions for help from relatives or government and nonprofit agencies.
- Required pre-purchase educational session.
- Relaxed qualifying guidelines that recognize non-traditional sources of income and wealth and use a history of rent-paying to establish credit rating.

Those who originate mortgages will provide homeowners with loans that conform to the guidelines of secondary purchasers.

The regional Federal Home Loan Banks are mandated to devote a certain portion of their funds to affordable housing programs. To do this, the banks award grants to local lenders who devise special lending programs tailored to the needs in their market area. These programs may offer special low interest rates, low down payment requirements or cash assistance, or relaxed qualifying guidelines. In most cases, eligibility is restricted to first-time buyers with incomes below a specified amount. Information on the availability of these loans can be obtained by contacting the Home Loan Bank in your region (most have Web pages; search on "Federal Home Loan Bank").

Local and state governments offer special mortgage loan programs for first-time homebuyers. These loans carry below-market interest rates. Borrowers must not have owned a home in the last three years nor have an income above a specified amount (which varies according to the local median income). The government funds these loans by issuing municipal bonds that sell at low yields because interest is exempt from federal income tax.

All of these loans are originated by regular mortgage lenders: banks, thrifts, mortgage bankers, and brokers. The agency or company sponsoring the loan either provides insurance or buys the loan once it is originated.

Therefore, you can obtain information about what is available in your area by asking local lenders. Alternatively, you may want to contact the housing department of your city or county to find out what help they can offer. In addition, you may be able to get a list of approved lenders from the FHA, Fannie Mae, Freddie Mac, or your local housing office.

There are a number of nonprofit organizations that help eligible homebuyers come up with cash for down payments and closing costs and may even provide below-market-interest-rate loans. Some of these programs are nationwide, such as the Neighborhood Assistance Corporation of America, AmeriDream, Newsong, the Nehemiah Program, and Neighborhood Gold. Many municipalities also conduct programs funded by grants from state governments or through the use of special municipal bond issues.

If you fall into a category that might qualify you for assistance, such as being a first-time buyer (or if you haven't owned for a number of years) or having income below the local median income (check the Census Bureau or your local HUD office to see what that is), it may be worthwhile to search for special loan programs that you can access. An especially good source of information is the local housing counseling agency, which not only provides information, but also offers educational courses to help you become eligible. A list of HUD-approved agencies is available at *www.hud.gov/offices/hsg/sfh/hcc/hccprof14.cfm.*

If you plan to buy a house sometime in the future, but not immediately, a good way to save up a down payment is to put money in a Roth Individual Retirement Account (Roth IRA). For years 2005–2007, you can invest up to $4,000* per year in the account. Although you must pay tax on the money invested, all earnings and appreciation are tax-free. So, when you take the

---

*More if you are over 50 years of age, under a "catch-up" provision.

money out, you will pay no taxes on it. Ordinarily, you cannot touch the money until you are 59½ years old, but with a Roth, you can withdraw the money to make a down payment on a first home purchase without penalty as long as the account is at least five years old. Check with your tax advisor for more details. At the time of publication, the Bush administration proposed an expansion of the Roth IRA program, as well as a broader program for tax-free savings accounts.

12

LOAN APPLICATION PROCESS

Once you have settled on a lender and the type of loan you want, it is time to make a formal application. The time between application and loan approval may be two to eight weeks. This is a time of anxiety for many borrowers, especially if there is some question as to whether they can qualify for the loan. Even for those who easily qualify, the delay can be frustrating.

It may help to understand what the lender is doing during this time. The lender's most important task is to assess the risk involved in granting the loan. The lender must also prepare the necessary documentation on the loan to satisfy government regulators and investors who may purchase the loan.

The lender will order a credit report, which shows your history of meeting financial obligations. Problems may occur if you have defaulted on loans and credit agreements in the past, or if you have yet to establish a credit record. In most cases, the lender will refer to a "score" based on the information in your credit report. These scores are often referred to as FICO scores, a reference to the Fair Isaac Company that pioneered the development of credit scores. Your score will determine whether you are granted a loan and the terms that will be offered. Some lenders will make a loan to an applicant with a low score, but the interest rate and required down payment will vary greatly according to your score. The lender will also verify information you have provided on income, employment, and bank accounts. This information is needed to see if you qualify for the loan (see Key 9).

The lender also orders an appraisal of the property. This is used to verify that the property is worth at least as much as you agreed to pay for it. The loan-to-value ratio is applied to the *lesser* of the contract price or market value. If you are buying a house, the loan will be a percentage of its appraised value or its cost, whichever is less.

In addition to the lender's work, it must be approved if the loan is for more than 80% of the value determined by FHA, VA, or a private insurer. This may add some time to the approval process.

When all information is in, the application is presented to the loan approval committee. This committee meets periodically to endorse or reject the recommendations of the loan officer. If your application is approved, you can proceed with the closing. If not, you must start over with another lender.

Recently, some lenders have been trying to gain a competitive edge by offering quick loan approval through less documentation than has been required in the past. Traditional requirements and newly devised ones are compared below. Some lenders will use the method more suitable for you.

Traditional	*New Alternatives*
Verify employment	* Two years' W-2 statements, and
	* current paycheck stub with year-to-date earnings
Verify deposits	* Three months' savings and checking account deposits
Verify mortgage	* Credit report reference for last six months, or
	* six months' mortgage payment history, or
	* canceled checks for last year

Technology continues to transform the ways in which loan applications are submitted and evaluated. Today, you can start the loan application process over the Internet or in a real estate broker's office. Many lenders use automated systems to analyze the risk of making the loan. The major loan purchasing firms, Fannie Mae and Freddie Mac, operate computerized loan underwriting systems with their criteria built in. If the loan passes the test, there is no need for a loan approval committee. As a result of these advances, the time required to approve a loan is shrinking. This is good news for homebuyers waiting for the go-ahead to complete a purchase. Ultimately, this trend will bring down the costs of securing a loan, as well.

13

LOANS THAT REQUIRE LESS PAPERWORK

When lenders provide a large amount of money to buy a home, they want to know as much about your finances as they can. After all, they want to know that their investment is sound and that you will live up to your part of the bargain. However, there are some lenders who are willing to forgo much of the information gathering for a price. And when house prices are going up and markets are vibrant, as they were in the early years of the twenty-first century, this type of loan is readily available and popular with borrowers.

As indicated in Key 12, loan applications generally require three types of information: your employment and income, your current debt and financial resources, and the property you are buying. "No-doc" and "low-doc" loans dispense with most of the information about employment and income, relying on statistics like your credit score to assess your likelihood of repaying the loan. You will still have to get a credit report, with a FICO score calculated, and have an appraisal done of the property. But most of the information that borrowers usually must supply from their personal records or have their employers supply will not be needed or will be reduced in volume.

What type of borrower is attracted to low-documentation loans? There may be several reasons why someone would desire to reduce the personal information supplied:

- The information is onerous to collect, or the papers are not readily available and have to be collected at significant trouble and expense.

- The borrower does not want to alert his employer that he is applying for a loan.
- The borrower is self-employed and verifying income is difficult. Often, a small business owner will have somewhat variable income, and the results of the past few years might not be indicative of future income.
- The borrower may have income sources he does not wish to divulge. These may include disreputable or even illegal activities.
- The borrower cannot qualify for a conforming loan, but is willing to take on high debt payments.

Most lenders who process loan applications do not intend to hold the loan. It is the secondary investors, largely Fannie and Freddie, who establish the requirements for the information gathered on mortgage loans. There is little incentive for these big loan buyers to reduce their requirements. However, those who buy "nonconforming" loans can set whatever standards they want. And often they will reduce the requirements so as to increase their holdings of mortgage loans, particularly when these loans appear secure regardless of the credit history of the borrowers. A large percentage of loans held in portfolios not owned by Fannie and Freddie are reduced-documentation loans. For the additional risk connected with these loans, lenders get a slightly higher interest rate—one-quarter to one full percentage point—and may require a lower loan-to-value ratio. They are probably more appropriate as a source of refinancing to reduce the existing interest rate on a loan than as a way to finance the initial purchase of a house. The relative speed and certainty of loan approval may be important in these instances.

14

GUARANTEED AND INSURED LOANS

A key to buying a home is arranging a loan that is large enough. The standard mortgage loan covers 80% of the purchase price of the home, so the home buyer must supply a cash down payment of 20% of the price. Obviously, the size of this required payment presents a serious barrier to many people trying to buy a first home.

Fortunately, mortgage loans for more than 80% are commonly available. There are government agencies and private companies willing to insure or guarantee the amount of loan over the standard.

The Federal Housing Administration routinely provides mortgage insurance for loans up to 97% of the value of the home. (The loan may cover most of the closing costs, as well.) These *FHA loans* can be obtained from the same lenders who make standard loans. When you apply for the loan, you also apply for FHA insurance. If you default on the loan, the FHA reimburses the lender for any loss up to the amount covered by the insurance.

FHA programs are intended to help low- and moderate-income people buy homes. For that reason, there is a limit to the size of loan the FHA may insure. (To find the maximum loan for your county, go to the Internet at *http://entp.hud.gov/idapp/html/hicostlook.cfm* and enter the name of your county or metropolitan area.) For loans that are less restrictive, you may apply for insurance from a private mortgage insurance company. These programs work much like FHA insurance and are commonly called *PMI loans.*

If you are a military veteran, you may be eligible for a VA loan. The Department of Veterans Affairs provides qualified veterans with an entitlement you can use to obtain a loan for up to 100 percent of the value of the home. The amount of the entitlement depends on your military service and your previous VA loans. It is possible to get a loan for as much as $417,000 with no down payment.

Although the VA guarantee is provided free of charge to qualified veterans, there are some closing costs on the loan. Loans insured by the FHA or guaranteed by the VA are called *government-backed loans.* All other loans, even those insured through private mortgage insurance, are called *conventional loans.*

Mortgage insurance requires payment by the borrower of a premium. In most cases, part of this premium is paid in a lump sum at the loan closing and part is added to each monthly loan payment. Other features of FHA and VA loans are:

- FHA and VA loans are assumable. This means you may be able to sell the house with the new owner keeping the same interest rate. The FHA applies minimal credit requirements to the person assuming the loan. Today, credit approval is necessary. If you have a VA loan and the buyer assumes it, you may lose your entitlement. However, buyers who are veterans may be able to substitute their entitlement for the seller's. This means that the seller can obtain another VA loan in the future.

- Government-guaranteed loans, especially FHA loans, require more time for approval than conventional loans, adding several weeks to your loan application process. FHA and VA loans can be used for refinancing. You need not be purchasing a home to get the loan.

- The rate of interest charged on FHA loans is somewhat higher than that charged on conventional loans. When comparing rates, ask for the FHA rate.

- FHA loans may be easier to obtain. The ratios applied to income and debt are higher, meaning that a borrower could secure a larger loan for the same amount of income. In addition, FHA generally shows more leniency when reviewing a borrower's credit history.

15

CANCELING OR AVOIDING PRIVATE MORTGAGE INSURANCE

In general, if you do not make a cash down payment of at least 20% of the home's value, you must arrange for some type of mortgage insurance. There are two basic choices: government insurance through the FHA or insurance from a private company. The latter is commonly referred to as PMI (Private Mortgage Insurance) and is similar to, yet different from, FHA insurance.

With either FHA or PMI, you do not have to go out and shop for the insurance. You merely tell the lender you want an FHA loan or a "conventional" loan. A conventional loan will be insured by a PMI company if the lender so requires. The lender applies for the insurance when you apply for the loan. The loan will not be provided if the insurance is not approved. The insurance will compensate the lender for losses incurred should you default on the loan and the lender is forced to foreclose. You pay the insurance premiums and benefit by being able to borrow more that 80% of the cost of the home.

A number of factors affect the amount of premium you must pay for PMI, and some of them are within your control. Others are determined by the lender and the type of loan you select. Therefore, it makes sense to ask about PMI premiums when comparing loan terms. Some lenders may require more coverage, and that will drive up the cost. Premiums are usually higher for adjustable-rate mortgages (ARMS) than they are for fixed-rate loans. They may be higher for longer-term loans. Premiums also increase substantially as the loan-to-value (LTV) ratio increases. For example, if you make a 10%

down payment (LTV of 90%), your premiums will be lower than someone making only a 5% down payment.

There are different ways you can pay the premium, and your choice will affect the premium amount. Paying one lump sum at closing will usually give you the lowest total premium because it ignores the time value of money. However, if you want the right to a partial refund in case you prepay the loan (a highly likely possibility), it will cost extra. You can also pay the premium on an annual basis, with or without the option of a refund for the part of the year after you prepay the loan. Alternatively, you can pay as you go in a series of monthly payments. The latter is probably a good choice if you think you may move or pay off the loan within a few years of purchase.

You can cancel PMI when the balance of the loan is less than 80% of the value of the home. Two conditions make this possible. First, you are paying the loan off very gradually, so the balance declines slightly with each payment. Second, in ideal situations, the value of your home is increasing. You can determine the balance of the loan at any time by consulting an amortization table for your loan. But, because the value of the home can be documented only through a professional appraisal, you will have to spend money (about $400) on an appraisal to verify that your home has increased in value. You may point to a tax assessment, which you get free from the local tax assessor, but remember that assessments are often below the true market value of the home, so the assessed value may not support your point. You can also argue that the value of your home has at least remained constant and try to get the insurance canceled based purely on amortization.

In 1999, the Homeowners' Protection Act was passed by Congress in an effort to make it easier to cancel PMI. The law requires lenders to notify borrowers of their right to cancel and the procedure required to do so. Further, if the mortgage balance is less than 78% of the current value of the house (based on amortization), the insurance is automatically canceled. The law applies to loans closed after July of **1999,** so check to see if you are eligible. Some lenders are extending these benefits to borrowers with loans made before the effective date.

There are ways to avoid PMI altogether. One is by securing an FHA loan. The main constraint is the cap placed on FHA loan amounts, although that maximum has expanded greatly in recent years. (The FHA limit is 48% of the maximum on conventional loans that can be purchased by Fannie Mae. In 2006, this worked out to be $200,160 for a single-family home. In high-cost areas, an FHA loan can go up to 87% of the conventional limit, or $362,790 for a single-family unit in 2006 terms.) However, FHA loans have their own insurance premiums, which may be as high as or higher than PMI payments. If you are a military veteran, you may qualify for a loan guarantee from the Department of Veterans Affairs that allows you to buy a home with a very small down payment. Also, there are no premiums for the guarantee.

The FHA has a provision similar to that of PMI loans that allows cancellation of mortgage premiums after the loan is paid down below 78% of the original value. Barring supplemental payments to principal, it takes a long time to reduce outstanding debt through normal amortization (if you have made extra payments, you must apply for cancellation, and the loan must be at least five years old). In almost all cases, a homeowner would have refinanced or sold the home before the outstanding principal drops below 78% of the original value (increases in the home's value do not count). However, there is one thing you should know about FHA insurance. If you do refinance or sell the home, resulting in the loan being retired, you may be able to obtain a refund of part of the upfront premium you paid at origination. A lot of people do not apply for this refund, so ask the lender when you pay off the loan.

If the lender agrees, you can use another loan to make part of the down payment. This second mortgage that supplies cash to substitute for the bulk of the down payment will carry a higher interest rate than the first mortgage. But there is no requirement for insurance on the second loan and, if the first loan is for no more than 80% of value, there should be no insurance requirement for that loan either. Such a combination of loans may be arranged from a lending institution or through a mortgage broker. These are often referred to as "80-10-10" loans or some other combination of numbers. The first number indicates the percentage of value represented by the first mortgage, the second number is the percentage for the second mortgage, and the last number is the percentage of the cash down payment. Thus, an "80-15-5" loan requires a 5% down payment. Note that the combined payment for the two loans may be more than the payment for an insured loan, including the premium. However, interest paid on the second mortgage can be deducted from taxable income if you itemize, while FHA or PMI premiums cannot. In addition, when the second loan is retired, typically after 5 to 10 years, you will have a lower loan balance than if you had taken out one large loan.

16

SELLER FINANCING

A property seller may assist a buyer by providing some or all of the financing needed. In some cases a small, second mortgage may be extended, but when bank loans are unavailable, the seller may have to provide most of the purchase price by accepting a mortgage.

There are two principal reasons for a seller to consider extending a home mortgage loan:

1. Institutional lenders are unwilling to finance the sale. You may be able to extend favorable loan terms and an interest rate to rescue the sale.
2. By providing favorable financing, you may get a higher price for the property.

There are two principal reasons for a buyer to consider seller financing:

1. To be able to negotiate a larger loan with favorable mortgage terms.
2. Mortgage clauses, including payment timing, payment structuring, personal liability, and prepayment options, can be negotiated to suit the buyer's requirements.

The major terms and considerations of typical seller financing are:

Length of Mortgage. Since the seller generally does not want to wait 25 or 30 years for the money and the buyer wants to avoid the high monthly payments associated with a short-term loan, a *balloon mortgage is* used. The monthly payments are based on a 25-year amortization schedule, but the entire loan matures (balloons) in a relatively short period of time. This time period ranges from a few months up to ten years.

Loan-To-Value Ratio. The seller generally wants a large cash down payment so that the loan is more secure, while the buyer wants to make a small down payment to retain as much cash as possible. A minimum of 10% down is frequently agreed upon.

Loan Prepayment. The buyer must be able to have the right to prepay the loan without penalty when new financing can be arranged. The seller may want this same condition to get the money back sooner. However, the seller may not have a better use for the money and therefore prefer that the loan not be paid off early unless there is a prepayment penalty.

Interest Rate. This is a good bargaining point. If the rate is below the rate on available loans, expect to get a good price for the property.

Right to Assign. With this right, if the initial borrower sells the property during the term of the loan, the new buyer may assume the existing note without the lender's consent.

Tax Considerations. Periodic payments result in interest deductions for the borrower each year, but taxable income for the note holder.

Non-recourse. If arranged, this limits the buyer's loss to the amount of equity; no personal liability on the loan.

Frequently, a lot or vacant land purchased for development involves seller financing. With this arrangement, the seller accepts a small (10 to 20%) cash down payment and the buyer's note (secured by a first mortgage on the property) for the unpaid balance of the price. The loan is usually paid off by a construction loan.

17

DISCOUNT POINTS AND INTEREST RATES

When you shop for a loan, you should look at more than the interest rate alone. Mortgage loans usually require the payment of discount points in addition to the various fees associated with originating the loan. These points are additional interest paid at the time the loan is closed and can add substantially to the cost of the loan. When the lender quotes an interest rate, it is usually expressed as "eight percent plus two points."

Each point is a charge of 1% of the amount of the loan. For example, if you are seeking a loan of $98,000, one point would cost you $980. At the closing, the lender will advance only $97,020 ($98,000 less $980), and you must make up the difference. Alternatively, you can write a check to the lender for $980 and the lender will advance the full amount. There is no real difference, except for tax purposes. If you write a check for the points, you should be entitled to an immediate tax deduction for the points, provided you are getting the mortgage to buy a principal residence (refinancing will not qualify) and that the points are a customary charge in your local area.

In either case, your loan payments are based on the full $98,000, and that is how much principal you will eventually pay back to the lender. This means you must come up with additional cash to buy the home or to refinance an existing loan. In some cases of refinanced loans, the lender will allow you to borrow the points and pay them back as part of the monthly payments. You should take this expense into account when deciding whether or not to refinance.

Within the loan market, there probably will be a variety of combinations of interest rates and points. The same lender may offer different combinations. If you are short of cash, you should look for loans with no or few discount points. However, these loans will probably carry higher interest rates. If you are having trouble qualifying for the loan, you may wish to pay more points for a lower interest rate. Many lenders allow you to pay additional points to reduce the interest rate further. These types of loans are called *buy-downs*. You may even try to negotiate with the seller of the home to pay some or all of the points.

If you are indifferent as to whether you pay the cost of the loan in the form of points or a higher interest rate, you will want to compare loan offerings on the basis of actual cost. When the points are factored into the cost of the loan, the rate is called the *effective interest rate*. The lender's disclosure of the true cost of the loan should indicate the *annual percentage rate* (APR). This is the effective interest rate assuming you keep the loan until it is paid off. As a rule of thumb, each discount point adds approximately one-eighth of one percentage point to the interest rate. This can be seen by referring to the chart below.

Effective Interest Rates
for 30-Year Loans Held to Maturity

Interest Rate	Discount Points			
	1	2	3	4
6%	6.09	6.19	6.29	6.39
7%	7.10	7.20	7.30	7.41
8%	8.11	8.21	8.32	8.44
9%	9.11	9.23	9.34	9.46
10%	10.12	10.24	10.37	10.50
11%	11.12	11.25	11.38	11.52
12%	12.14	12.28	12.42	12.56
13%	13.14	13.29	13.43	13.58

As the chart indicates, a loan at 10% interest and four points has the same effective interest rate as one at 10.5% interest and no points. These comparisons are for loans held for the entire 30 years to maturity. If the loan is held for a shorter time, the effective rate will be higher, depending on how long the loan is outstanding. Differences are not too great for loans that go beyond ten years, but they are for loans paid much earlier.

For example, a 10% loan with two points that is pre-paid in one year has an effective rate of 12% because the two points are all returned in just one year; so, the two points can be added to the 10% annual interest rate. If that loan is outstanding for two years, the two points are spread over two years; so the annual interest rate is about 11% (10% interest plus one point each year). As you can see, the idea is to spread the points over the life of the loan. However, points are not spread evenly, owing to a complicated computation of the effective interest rate.

18

REFINANCING MORTGAGES

Even though most mortgage loans are originated for a term of 25 to 30 years, few borrowers keep the loan for more than 5 to 10 years. In many cases, mortgages are paid off when the home is sold. However, many home owners refinance their loans, and for many reasons. A key advantage of being a mortgage borrower is the ability to change financing as conditions change.

Refinance when you need to raise money for some purpose. Over time, you accumulate equity in your home. Equity is the difference between the value of the home and how much you owe on the mortgage. Essentially, your home equity is a form of personal wealth, just like stocks and bonds. Equity increases as the value of your home rises. It also increases as you gradually pay off the principal of the mortgage loan.

Often, until you sell the home, this equity is locked in. Fortunately, you can access equity by refinancing the old loan for one with a higher principal or by getting an additional mortgage on the home. You may find that a loan secured by your home equity is less expensive than other types of consumer loans. Both the interest rate and repayment term are more favorable than other types of borrowing. There are also tax advantages to using a home loan, as compared to other types of borrowing.

A great reason to refinance a loan is to take advantage of lower interest rates. For example, suppose you have a fixed-rate loan that you obtained when interest rates were high. You may find that you can get a new loan at a lower rate of interest. A home owner can significantly reduce monthly payments using this tactic.

You may have had a loan provided by the seller when you bought your home. Most of these loans have terms that "balloon," or expire in a few years. By refinancing, you can assure yourself of long-term financing for your home.

In other cases, home owners with adjustable-rate mortgages (ARMS) may want to refinance with fixed-rate loans while interest rates are relatively low. In this way, the borrower can lock in the interest rate and avoid the risk of rates rising in the future.

If you have major improvements made to your home, you may want to refinance to pay for the work. The improvements should increase the value of the home and allow you to get a larger loan. Even though you can finance improvements in other ways, a new loan covering the entire home might be the least expensive alternative.

Finally, refinancing may be helpful before you sell your home. When rates are low, you may obtain a loan that can be assumed by the buyer. If rates increase before you sell, or if mortgage loans become hard to obtain, an assumable loan can add to the resale value of your home.

There are certain costs associated with refinancing. Your existing loan may have prepayment penalties that must be paid if the loan is paid back early. The new loan will require application fees, various charges, and discount points. These costs must be considered in the decision to refinance. Any savings from the refinancing must outweigh the costs. These savings will be realized over the period you have the loan, so you must stay in the house long enough to make refinancing worthwhile.

19

TOTAL COST
OF THE LOAN

A fundamental key to selecting the best loan is to consider total costs, not just the interest rate. This will include monthly payments and the cash required at closing.

Almost all mortgage loans require monthly payments of principal and interest. This is the amount indicated in monthly payment tables. However, this is only part of the total cost of the loan. There are other charges that must be paid "up front" or as part of the monthly payments.

When you apply for a loan, you are required to pay an application fee. This fee usually amounts to several hundred dollars. A portion goes toward obtaining information on your credit history so the lender can evaluate your credit. Another portion goes to pay for an appraisal of the home for assurance that the home is worth at least as much as you are paying. If the appraised value is lower, the amount of loan you are applying for may be reduced. The rest of the application fee goes to defray the costs of processing your application or toward the lender's profit.

When the loan closes (this is done simultaneously with the closing of the new purchase), there are other amounts you must pay. The biggest is the down payment or the difference between the loan amount and the price of the home. Think of that as an investment, not a loan cost. The down payment establishes your equity in the home at the time you take ownership. If all goes well, you will recover this, with some profit, when you sell in the future.

If the loan requires payment of discount points, these are due at the closing. Each point costs 1% of the amount of the loan. This money goes to the lender to increase the income from making the loan. No one knows for sure why mortgage loans are priced this way (instead of just using an interest rate with no discount). It is traditional, and virtually all mortgage lenders charge points. One or more discount points may be considered "loan origination fees." The effect of these fees is the same as discount points. However, they are often separated out, and the terminology determines the income tax implications. Discount points for a purchase loan may be deducted on your tax return as mortgage interest, whereas origination fees are not tax deductible. When getting quotes on current loan terms, recognize that when points are reported as "2 plus 1" or "2/1," that means three points, one of which is a loan origination fee.

Other expenses at closing involve services that the lender requires. A survey indicates the exact size and boundaries of the lot and verifies that there are no encroachments by adjoining properties. A title insurance policy is required to protect against legal claims against the property. A hazard and liability insurance policy must be purchased and maintained on the home. If there is mortgage insurance, a premium may be due at closing or added to the monthly payment, or both. Many private mortgage insurance companies offer a variety of ways of paying the Mortgage Insurance Premium (MIP). Most borrowers opt for a monthly payment with no premium at closing. For FHA loans, there is a premium due at closing (1.5% at the time of publication) and an additional monthly MIP for loans over 90% of value. You can fold the up-front MIP into the loan and pay it off monthly.

Most lenders require you to maintain an escrow account. The purpose of this account is to pay property taxes and hazard insurance premiums as they come due each year. The amount needed annually is estimated and divided equally by 12 months. The total monthly payment is often referred to as "PITI"—principal, interest, taxes, and insurance. While these expenses would be incurred even if you did not use financing, maintenance of an escrow account denies you use of the money during the year. The assessments are made before the expenses are due, and only rarely is any interest paid on the actual escrow accumulation.

Total payments on the loan are not the same as total costs. A 30-year loan may require twice the amount in payments as a 15-year loan, but the true cost in today's dollars may be the same, depending on the rate of inflation over the terms of the loans.

20

LOAN QUALIFYING

Among the things that have changed in recent years is the way loan applicants are qualified for mortgage loans. Loan officers used to calculate a set of ratios based on an applicant's income and existing debt obligations. If income was too low relative to the loan payment, the loan was denied. The applicant would then have to either find a lower-priced home or come up with more down payment cash. Today, lenders rely much more on credit scores and other factors to make the loan decision and may not even calculate income ratios. However, that does not mean that these ratios are not a good way to determine whether you can afford a loan. You may want to calculate your own ratios and compare them to the traditional standards rather than obligate yourself to a loan based on what the lender thinks you can afford.

This key shows how the ratios are calculated and is based on the standards formerly applied to conventional loans. You may want to use your own standards based on your personal budget. To do so, consider how much of your monthly income you are willing to devote to a house payment (realizing that the payment will remain constant, except for any tax and insurance included, over the long term while, hopefully, your income will increase) and use that ratio in your evaluation.

The best way to describe loan qualifying is with an example: Suppose the Browns apply for a mortgage loan of $150,000. The lenders then ask them to state their income. Mr. Brown makes $45,000 a year, and Mrs. Brown makes $30,000, bringing their total monthly income to $6,250. The loan is for 90% of value with a fixed rate of 8% (30 years). Monthly payments are $1,101 for principal and interest, plus $300 for escrow.

The lender divides the PITI by monthly income:

$1,401 ÷ $6,250 = 22.4%

This ratio is within the 28%* needed to qualify, so the loan looks affordable. Next the lender considers payments on other debts. The Browns pay auto loans of $600 per month, and a $250 monthly student loan. Adding these to the mortgage payment makes their total debt payments $2,251 per month:

$2,251 ÷ $6,250 = 36%

Because the debt ratio is right at the 36%* needed to qualify, they should qualify for the loan. This assumes that the Browns' credit rating or score is sufficient to entitle them to the best credit terms. A low rating might have disqualified them even though they passed the ratios. On the other hand, an excellent rating may encourage the lender to bend the ratios if necessary. Also be aware that some first-time homebuyer programs offer more liberal ratios. If the Browns are applying for an adjustable-rate loan, the lender may base the loan payment on a rate higher than that charged initially. This practice accounts for the likely increase in the rate after the first year of the loan.

If they were applying for an FHA loan, the criteria would change (even though $150,000 is more than the FHA can insure, we will use the same example). Since the FHA ratio of PITI to income should reach no more than 29%, and total debt payments no more than 41%, no problem arises here. In fact, they pass with more of a margin than in the conventional case.

The FHA uses a new way of calculating the maximum loan it will insure. A maximum percentage that

*These ratios apply to "conforming" loans. A conforming loan is one that is eligible for purchase by Fannie Mae or Freddie Mac. These agencies establish specific criteria for loans they purchase.

varies by the price of the home and whether it is located in an area with traditionally high or low closing costs is applied to the value (the lesser of the price or appraised amount) of the home. The up-front mortgage insurance premium (MIP) and closing costs can be financed into the loan, but the borrower is required to make a cash investment equal to at least 3% of total purchase costs.

The purpose of these qualifying ratios is to prevent making loans to people who will find it difficult to meet the payment obligation each month. You may consider the maximum payment allowed more burdensome than you would like, and there is no reason you must get a loan that large. You may want to look for a home that is more modest. However, you may feel comfortable taking on a payment burden even more onerous than the maximum allowed. In that case, if you can present an argument for the increase by pointing out any "compensating factors" that might indicate your ability to handle the extra debt, you might secure a larger loan. For example, if the home is newly constructed or is especially energy efficient, the lender might employ a higher ratio reflecting the likely lower maintenance cost. If you make a larger than normal down payment, you might get a larger loan relative to your income. If your record shows you paid a comparable amount of rent in a timely manner, the lender might allow a higher payment-to-income ratio.

Loans specially tailored for first-time homebuyers often allow higher ratios for both mortgage payment and total debt than other conventional loans. For some programs, the 28/36 percent ratios are extended to 33/38 percent. That means if you think you can qualify for one of these types of loans, you may expand your home search to a slightly more expensive range. On the other hand, if you are planning to use an Adjustable Rate Mortgage with less than a 10% down payment, the ratios will probably be lower (25/33 percent). That would narrow your range of houses a bit.

21

HOW A LOAN APPLICATION IS EVALUATED

Many years ago, each lender would evaluate your loan application independently, using criteria established by that lender. Several changes in the mortgage industry make that procedure untenable now. First, most loans originated by lenders are sold into the secondary market. Purchasers of these loans, most often either Fannie Mae or Freddie Mac, have their own standards for acceptable loans, and loan originators must meet those standards if they hope to sell their loans. Second, lenders were coming under fire for basing loan decisions on subjective characteristics of the borrowers, raising concerns about illegal discrimination. As long as it could be shown that ethnic minorities, women, and people living in poorer neighborhoods were being turned down for loans at a higher rate than others, the loan approval process was suspect. Third, technology allows the loan application process to be sped up, and lenders utilizing the Internet threaten to take significant market share from those who require a long time to approve loans. Fourth, pressures to expand the market create a need for ways to better distinguish good credit risks that are not dependent on personal judgment and traditional criteria.

Research at a company called Fair Isaac Company led to the development of a single number "score," now called a credit score or a FICO score, to estimate a person's ability to handle credit. The number itself is a weighted average of a number of factors thought to determine a person's likelihood of repaying a loan (credit scores are used for purposes other than loan risk evaluation—insurance companies also use them—and each score is custom-tailored to fit that application). The weights used to calculate the score are derived from statistics of past experience with loan repayment. A computer can be programmed to provide scores. A lender need only establish a policy for the minimum acceptable score for loan approval. Once an application is input into the computer, a "go/no go" decision can be quickly made. Since the data in the credit report does not include information that is considered discriminatory (race, sex, national origin), a decision based on a credit score is inherently less biased.

In the current mortgage market, your credit score does not just determine whether you get a loan; it also influences what you will pay for it. In general, the lower the score, the higher the interest rate charged. Some loans, like low-documentation loans, require scores near the top of the range (FICO scores go from 300 to 850, but anything under 600 may throw you into the undesirable "subprime" category, where interest rates are much higher than those most people get). The data for credit scores come from the three major credit bureaus; in 2006, these companies introduced "VantageScore" as an alternative to FICO. VantageScores range from 501 to 990, with anything over 900 qualifying the borrower for the best terms, while scores under 600 qualify for the worst. You can contact these companies to check on your credit report and score. You are entitled by law (the Fair and Accurate Credit Transactions Act) to see a copy of your report once per year without charge. However, you may have to pay a fee to get your credit score. Here are the Web sites for the credit agencies:

Equifax: *www.equifax.com*
Experian: *www.experian.com* (also see *freecreditreport. com*, which is affiliated with Experian)
TransUnion: www.transunion.com

Alternatively, you can get free reports from any or all of the three agencies through their official cooperative site at *https://www.annualcreditreport.com*, but these reports will not include your FICO score, for which there is an additional charge. (Some sites provide extensive information for a fee: *www.myfico.com* provides all three scores and reports for $45.)

Five types of information go into calculating a credit score. The most important are your **payment history** and the **amounts you owe**. Of lesser importance are the **length of time** you have used credit, **new credit** accounts, and the **type of credit accounts** you have.

Payment history refers to how well you have handled credit in the past. Performance not only includes avoiding default—no collection agencies or bankruptcies—but also how timely you are in paying your bills. Consistently paying late will be reflected in your score. If you have had problems paying bills, or even a bankruptcy, the longer ago it was and the better your more recent performance has been, the less it will lower your score.

Creditors also are interested in the amount of debt you carry. If you carry a high balance on your accounts, you may not be in a good position to take on more debt. The level of payment on these accounts is considered as well in qualifying you for the loan because most lenders do not like to make loans to someone whose current obligations eat up too much of their income.

The longer you have used credit successfully, the better your score. Some people will buy something on credit when they are starting out even though they have the cash to pay for it. Taking out a loan that you know you can repay and then repaying it is a good way to establish a credit record and make it easier to get a loan at a later date. A large number of applications for new credit will downgrade a score. The implication is that you are seeking as many credit outlets as you can get to juggle a large amount of debt as it comes due. However, only recent applications are considered. If a large amount of your debt is in credit cards, your score will be lowered.

It is one thing to know what makes up your score but it is more useful to know how you can improve your score. There are things you can do to improve your chances of getting credit, but the information used in a credit score is accumulated over time and there is little you can do at the last minute. After all, the lender wants to know your historical pattern of using credit. If you have had problems but resolved to do better, they want some consistent performance to support your case. That said, here are some things you can do to help your score:

- Pay bills on time and stay current on your accounts. Resist the temptation to pay the minimum payment on credit card accounts.
- Get a copy of your credit report and challenge any information you know to be incorrect.
- Try to keep credit card balances as low as possible. Lenders consider anything less than 25% of total credit available to be good.
- Pay off any debt you can without using up your emergency reserves. The best strategy is to pay down credit card balances but not close the accounts. Lenders look at the ratio of your debt to total credit available, so closing an account only reduces your credit and increases the debt-to-credit ratio for the same amount of debt.
- Do not open a lot of new accounts. The increased credit available is offset by the activity of opening the accounts. Lenders are concerned that you will soon max out debt and skip town.
- Do not routinely open credit accounts. Stores often give discounts on purchases if you open a new account there. The discount might not be worth it if it reduces your credit score. On the other hand, rate shopping—checking available rates at a number of lenders—will not reduce your score even if the lenders check your credit as a condition of giving you a quote. The scoring methodology dismisses these types of inquiries as a normal part of search-ing for the best deal. Requesting a copy of your credit report also does not impact your score.

22

MORTGAGE LOANS FOR PEOPLE WITHOUT GOOD CREDIT

In the old days, mortgage lenders either granted your loan application or rejected it. If you were approved, you got the interest rate and terms currently offered by the lender. If you weren't approved, you got nothing. Today, approval of your loan application is not so much in doubt. However, the quality of your credit rating will have a lot to do with the terms you get on the loan. In the past, only applicants with good credit ratings were approved. Now, there is a loan for almost every applicant, but the costs vary.

People with high FICO scores get the best terms available. Those a notch or two down get less favorable terms—a slightly higher interest rate, a lower maximum loan-to-value ratio, higher required PMI. Those with the lowest scores are relegated to the world of "subprime" loans. Not all lenders make these high-risk loans. However, they can be found either through a mortgage broker or with a search of the Internet.

Subprime loans carry much higher interest rates—4 or 5 percentage points above the rate available to the best credit scores—and may require 5 or more front-end discount points on top of that. They may also require more documentation during the loan approval process. In addition, people seeking subprime loans may be vulnerable to "predatory" lending.

There are lenders who attempt to take advantage of borrowers who they think are inexperienced and unsophisticated in the ways of finance. Often, these are the same people who must resort to subprime loans. The expectation that you are not eligible for the loans made by mainstream lenders can make you less troubled by the tactics used by predatory lenders. At the same time, some of the methods termed "predatory" are merely attempts by the lender to reduce the risks of making subprime loans. That is why efforts to eliminate predatory lending have often floundered; the problem is defining what loan features should be outlawed.

The key for someone with poor credit who wants to buy a house is to know that there are subprime loans with terms that, while unfavorable compared to those of high-quality loans, are not predatory. Here are some of the practices and loan features that have been identified as predatory:

- The lender frequently pressures the borrower to refinance the loan with little benefit to the borrower. The lender, however, collects high fees at each refinancing.
- The lender guides the borrower into a subprime loan even though the borrower could qualify for a better loan.
- The lender charges fees much higher than the norm for the market. In addition, extra services of dubious value—such as loan life insurance—are required as a condition of making the loan.
- The loan involves negative amortization to the extent that unless the house increases in value rapidly, the borrower will end up owing more than the house is worth. The borrower ends up having difficulty in refinancing or selling the house and is trapped in the loan.
- The lender requires a prepayment penalty beyond the first three years of the loan term. Legitimate lenders use these penalties to recoup their sales costs in case interest rates fall and the borrower refinances. After a few years, however, the lender has received enough payments on the loan that a refi-

nancing is not a problem. Requiring the penalties on seasoned loans is a way to trap the borrower in a loan with unfavorable terms.

For the most part, predatory lending depends on a victim who is unaware of the options when shopping for a loan. Subprime borrowers may think they have no options and be relieved to find they can get a loan of any sort. Most of the time, however, the loan market is highly competitive, and it pays to search for the best deal. Because knowledge is crucial in discontinuing lender predation, laws intended to stop the practice focus on borrower awareness and education. Federal law—the Homeownership and Equity Protection Act of 1994— requires lenders who make "high-cost" loans to make specific disclosures. A high-cost loan is one that carries an interest rate at least 8 percentage points above the market rate. The disclosures alert the borrower that the loan is high-cost and that failure to live up to the terms of the loan may result in loss of the home (a lot of predatory loans are made to people who already own a home, but need cash for some reason). The law also lists practices and loan features that are not allowed on high-cost loans. In addition, several states have similar or stricter laws governing high-cost mortgage loans.

Subprime loans are for people who really want to buy a home or need to pull cash out of a home they already own, but do not have good enough credit to access the best loan terms. The fact that the mortgage market offers such financing makes housing markets more efficient and provides opportunities for more people to become homeowners. It could be argued that the pressure to meet the obligations of a mortgage loan can provide the discipline needed by some to improve their credit history and perhaps lead to their qualifying for low-cost loans in the future. If you fall into the category of subprime borrower, good knowledge of what is available and the tactics of unscrupulous lenders is essential to avoid the trap of predatory lending.

23

CO-SIGNING
A MORTGAGE

Suppose you want to apply for a mortgage loan, but you are just starting out and have no established credit history, or you have gone through a bankruptcy and your credit is damaged. In either case, you feel that you will be able to build up a good credit rating in the future, but for the present you need the loan. You find that the only loan a lender will give you—a subprime loan—is unaffordable because of the high interest rate and closing costs. Are you completely out of luck?

Actually, there is a way you may be able to qualify for a loan with reasonable terms. You may be able to persuade a parent or other relative or a very good friend to co-sign the loan documents. If the co-signer's credit is good, the lender may be willing to substitute that person's credit rating for your own and grant the loan on that basis. Conversely, you may encounter a situation where you are asked to co-sign a mortgage loan for a friend or relative.

In either case, it is important to recognize that co-signing a loan is a much larger commitment than merely vouching for the borrower. The co-signer is, in effect, entering into the loan agreement with the borrower, almost as if a business partnership were being formed. The co-signer takes on all the responsibilities of the borrower (and most often without any of the benefits). If the borrower fails to make the loan payments, or defaults in any other way, the lender may look to the co-signer to make good on the loan. Except where state law prohibits the practice, the lender can go after the co-signer without first bringing action against the borrower.

The best situation is when the co-signer is in sufficient financial condition to make the loan payments or pay off the loan if need be. The co-signer should have good reason to believe the borrower will make the payments faithfully. Co-signing for someone who is financially irresponsible is asking for trouble and actually is of little benefit to the borrower. A default could be costly and could damage the credit rating of the co-signer.

Here are some things a co-signer should do before committing:

- Federal law requires the lender to give you a booklet explaining your rights and obligations as a co-signer. Familiarize yourself with this information and make sure you are comfortable with the situation you are entering.
- Figure out how you will handle a default if it should occur. Do you have additional income to take on the payments and cash available for any fees and penalties incurred?
- Are you being asked to pledge any property—other than the mortgaged property—to the loan? Can you afford to lose that property?
- You should get all the papers involved with the mortgage loan, just as if you were the borrower. This includes all the legally required disclosures and information forms.
- Get an estimate of the amount you might owe if the loan defaults. Although this amount depends on when the default occurs, you might ask for a worst-case estimate.

Though it seems a hazardous thing to do, there may be times when co-signing a loan is warranted. It may be a way of giving a son or daughter a boost in acquiring a first home and may be more feasible than directly giving the child a large amount of cash. Perhaps a close friend is in a financial jam through no fault of his own, possibly after a serious illness or loss of a job. In the right situation, co-signing could be the right thing to do and provide a helping hand when it is most needed. In the wrong situation, it could become a disaster for all parties and place a severe strain on the relationship.

24

REFINANCING COSTS

Financial transactions can be costly, particularly if they involve mortgaging real property. In addition, getting a new loan may require as much time as it took to approve the original loan. These costs and delays should be considered in any refinancing decision.

If you are replacing an existing mortgage loan, there may be prepayment penalties. When you signed the mortgage note, you promised to pay back the loan according to the contract. However, most mortgage contracts contain a provision for repaying the loan early. This is called the "prepayment clause." Some loans require the payment of a penalty for early repayment. The amount is usually a percentage of the balance of the loan and may be reduced or eliminated after a specified period of time, typically five years. Check your loan contract or call the lender to see if a penalty applies. FHA and VA loans carry no penalties for prepayment. (See Key 34.)

Getting a new loan may involve the same types of costs as the original loan. These may include an application fee, discount points, credit check, home appraisal, survey, and title insurance policy. Together, these expenses may run several percentages of the amount of the loan. You may be able to eliminate some of these charges if you refinance with the same lender who holds your old loan. The lender has the right to charge you for all of these services but may waive some of them in the interest of keeping your loan.

If you are refinancing to obtain cash, you should consider the costs of refinancing when comparing loans from other sources. Borrowing against a home is usually a low-cost method in the long run, but for short-term financial needs there may be less expensive ways to get the money. Many home equity loans do not require full payment of these fees and charges, so you should shop aggressively.

What about refinancing loans advertised as requiring no costs? You can refinance with little or no out-of-pocket outlay, but the cost is masked by giving you an interest rate that is not as low as that on loans that do require some cash expense. You can find out what the real cost of the refinancing is by using the tables below. The body of the table has been rounded up to the next 0.125% because loans are offered in increments of 0.125%.

Comparable interest rate on loans with closing costs— "No-cost" loan at 6.5%

Loan Costs as % of Loan Amount	Expected Holding Period (years)		
	3	6	10
1	6.125	6.25	6.25
2	5.75	6	6.125
3	5.375	5.875	6
4	5	5.625	5.875
5	4.625	5.5	5.75

Comparable interest rate on loans with closing costs— "No-cost" loan at 7%

Loan Costs as % of Loan Amount	Expected Holding Period (years)		
	3	6	10
1	6.625	6.75	6.75
2	6.25	6.5	6.625
3	5.875	6.375	6.5
4	5.5	6.125	6.375
5	5.125	6	6.25

Comparable interest rate on loans with closing costs—
"No-cost" loan at 7.5%

Loan Costs as %	Expected Holding Period (years)		
of Loan Amount	3	6	10
1	7.125	7.25	7.25
2	6.75	7	7.125
3	6.375	6.875	7
4	6	6.625	6.875
5	5.625	6.5	6.75

Comparable interest rate on loans with closing costs—
"No-cost" loan at 8%

Loan Costs as %	Expected Holding Period (years)		
of Loan Amount	3	6	10
1	7.625	7.75	7.75
2	7.25	7.5	7.625
3	6.875	7.375	7.5
4	6.5	7.125	7.375
5	6.125	7	7.25

An example can be utilized to show how to use the table. Let's say that you find an offer for a loan that requires no closing costs when used to replace an existing mortgage loan. The loan is offered at 7.5% for 30 years. These loans are covered in the third table. You want to know how much lower the interest rate would have to be to justify paying costs out-of-pocket. Let's say you are willing to pay up to 4% of the loan amount in refinancing costs (points, fees, appraisals, and other costs charged to the borrower). Look on the row of the table corresponding to 4% costs. If you think you will pay off the loan (sell the house or refinance the loan) in 3 years, the comparable interest rate is 6%. If you expect to hold onto the loan for 10 years, the rate is 6.875%. If loans requiring 4% in costs have rates higher than these rates, the no-cost loan is a better deal. Of course, if you have no cash nor a way of borrowing the cash at a rate lower than 7.5 percent, the no-cost loan is the best choice, assuming the new rate is below the rate on your existing loan. Incidentally, why does it make a difference how long you hold the loan? Because the cost of refinancing is a one-time cost that is recovered (amortized) by a small savings each time you make a payment. The longer you hold the loan, the more savings you glean. The savings and the benefit of paying closing costs stop at the point that you retire the loan.

If you are refinancing to get a lower interest rate, the front-end costs of refinancing mean you must realize substantial savings in monthly payments to make the deal worthwhile. These savings come in the form of reduced monthly payments, so that you should consider how long you will likely remain in the home when considering the refinancing. You must remain with the home long enough to recover the costs of refinancing plus any income you could have made on the money spent. Key 48 shows you how to make this evaluation.

25

ESTIMATING INTEREST RATE ON NEW MONEY

In many refinancing situations, you may have the choice of two loan alternatives for different amounts. To compare the alternatives, you should know the cost of the additional money borrowed. Two examples are offered to illustrate this comparison.

Example 1. You need to raise $40,000 from the equity in your home. Should you get a new first mortgage to replace the existing one or add a second mortgage onto the existing mortgage?

You need to calculate the cost of the $40,000 cash raised. Suppose your old mortgage has a balance of $100,000, an interest rate of 6%, and 25 years to run. A new loan of $140,000 has an interest rate of 7% and runs for 25 years. Alternatively, you could get a second mortgage loan of $40,000 at 8% interest and keep the old loan.

First, you need to calculate the monthly payments under the new first mortgage loan. By referring to a table of mortgage payments such as those found on page 186 or in *Barron's Mortgage Payments*—available in book form at most libraries and book stores—you find the payment for a $140,000 loan at 7% and 25 years to be $989.49.* The payments on your existing loan are $644.30. Subtract the old from the new payment amount ($989.49 − $644.30 = $345.19). Now find a page in the tables where the payment for $40,000 (the additional

---

*If you have a financial calculator, see the section on "Use of Calculators" at the end of this book for instructions.

amount of the new loan) is close to the difference in payments ($345.19). When you find a match, look at the interest rate for that page of the table. The closest match in the table is $342.56 on page 195 for an interest rate of 9.25%. This is the effective interest rate of the new money. This shows that you could get a new $40,000 second mortgage loan at 9.25% and incur the same payments as if you refinanced the existing mortgage as described above.

The term periods of the loan were held constant in this example. The calculation gets more complex when the remaining terms of loans differ. Still, the key to understanding is that if you refinance at a higher rate to extract cash, the new rate will apply to the entire loan, not just the cash received.

Example 2. You can refinance your old mortgage at a lower rate of interest. The lender offers to finance the points in the new loan at a slightly higher rate of interest. Should you do this or pay in cash (or borrow the money elsewhere)?

Suppose you can refinance with a new $100,000 mortgage at 5% interest for 30 years. There are three discount points on the loan. If you wish to finance the cost of the points ($3000) into the new loan, the lender raises the interest rate to 5.25%. You want to calculate the cost of financing the points.

First, find the monthly payment for the new loan of $100,000 at 5%—$536.82 for a 30-year loan. Now, find the payment for a $103,000 loan ($100,000 plus cost of points) at 5.25%. This is $568.77. The difference in monthly payments is $31.95. You will find that a monthly payment of $32.02 on a loan of $3,000 for 30 years corresponds to a rate of 12.5%. If you can borrow the $3,000 elsewhere for less than 12.5%, you would be better off paying the points in cash. That is, provided the 12.5% (or less) rate includes all fees and charges.

To calculate this yourself, refer to the section on Use of Calculators, page 176.

26

COMPARING A NEW LOAN TO ADDED FINANCING

There are two basic ways to refinance when you need to "cash out" some equity. One, get a whole new first mortgage loan that is larger than the existing one by the amount of cash needed. Or two, get a second mortgage loan for the amount needed.

Choose the method that best fits your needs. From a personal viewpoint, if you plan to live in this home for the rest of your life, pay off the loan quickly. But if you're planning to move soon, put little in. Financially, a method for calculating the cost of borrowing additional money was described in Key 25 with an example that fits this problem.

Other considerations are:

- How much it will cost to refinance. These costs reduce the amount you will realize from the refinancing.
- What your monthly payments will be. The payments should fit within your monthly budget.
- How fast the loan will amortize. If you resell, the balance due on the loan must be deducted from your sales proceeds. A loan that pays off more quickly will leave you with more money after a sale.

As generalizations:

1. If your current first mortgage carries an above-market interest rate, then finance it by all means. You may pull out the cash, tax-free, while reducing the interest rate. Check the amount of any fees involved.

2. If your current first mortgage interest rate is at or below current market rates, you'll want to retain the first mortgage if possible. So, arrange a second mortgage.
3. One exception to no. 2 above is when the expected amount of cash you need is great (25% or more of the first mortgage). You may be better off refinancing the first mortgage, even at a somewhat higher interest rate, to avoid the high payments of a high-interest-rate, short-term second mortgage.

Also:

- Consider a home equity line of credit.
- Remember that if you get a second mortgage and anytime later want to replace the first mortgage through refinancing, the second mortgage will be promoted automatically by law to a first mortgage. In order to refinance the existing first mortgage, you will have to retire the second mortgage, often at a high cost.

For example, suppose your existing mortgage has a balance remaining of $165,000. The interest rate is 8% and the loan has 25 years left to run. Your current payment is $1,273.50 per month (this excludes the escrow payment). There is a prepayment penalty of 0.5% of the balance.

You need $30,000 in cash. You can get a new loan for $195,000 at 7% interest and two points. The loan is for 30 years. A second mortgage is available for $30,000 at 7.5% interest, two points, ten-year term.

If you take the new first mortgage loan, you must pay the prepayment penalty on your existing loan. This will cost $825 (.005 times $165,000). The points will run $3,900 (.02 times $195,000). The total cost is $4,725 plus other fees. If you get the second mortgage, you can avoid the prepayment penalty, but must pay the points for a cost of $600 plus other fees.

The monthly payment on the new loans can be found by using a mortgage table or financial calculator. The new first mortgage will have a payment of $1,297.34 (7% interest, 30 years, $195,000 principal). The second mortgage has a payment of $356.11 (7.5% interest, ten years, $30,000 principal). With the second mortgage, you will still be paying on the existing loan, so the total payment is $1,629.61 ($356.11 plus $1,273.50). The second mortgage alternative costs $332.27 more each month. It provides a benefit, that is the second mortgage is paid off over a shorter period of time.

27

TIME VALUE
OF MONEY

If you borrowed $ 100,000 to purchase a house and paid the loan back over 30 years at 10% interest, you would end up spending almost $320,000 on the loan. Some people think this is a good reason not to buy a home, since mortgage money is so "expensive." However, if you pay rent of $800 per month, you would pay $288,000 over 30 years, even if the rent did not go up during that time. Since it is likely that rents will increase within a 30-year span and the interest paid on the mortgage loan is tax deductible, the purchase option may be less expensive.

What makes the mortgage loan appear expensive when expressed in this way is ignoring the time value of money. Money received in the future must be *discounted* when compared to money received today. When discounted, we may speak of the money's *present value,* meaning the amount of money that would have to be invested today to equal the amount in the future. Although the example mortgage loan would require almost $320,000 in future payments, a lender would only pay $100,000 for the loan to get a 10% return. The loan's present value is $100,000.

There are several keys to understanding the time value of money:

Money today is worth more than money received in the future. If you have the money in hand, you can invest it and have more of it in the future. On the other hand, you may need to spend the money now. If you didn't have it, you would have to borrow it and pay back more in the future. In addition, whenever you invest money, there is a chance that you won't get it back, that you won't get back as much as you expected, or that inflation will decrease its value in the future. The further into the future you receive the money, the less valuable it is. At 10% interest, a $ 100 payment a year from now has a present value of almost $91, but the same payment two years from today has less than $83 of present value.

The amount by which money decreases in value in the future depends on the discount rate. This is equivalent to an interest rate. If the rate is high, the present value of future money is low (however, it should always have some positive value). If the rate is low, the present value is high (but never more than the amount in hand today). Discount rates differ from time to time and from person to person. If alternative investment opportunities are good, the rate will be relatively high. If the person lending the money has no immediate need for it, the rate will be lower. Risk also increases the rate. If the chance of repayment is low, the lender will demand a higher interest rate.

The effect of compound interest increases the return from an investment. Compounding means that interest is paid on interest that was earned and left on deposit. When the interest is earned and is reinvested, it earns interest along with the original principal. In effect, the interest earned becomes principal.

Consider the magic of compound interest: if you can earn 10% interest, compounded annually, $1000 deposited now will grow to more than $13.7 million in just 100 years!

A key to real estate finance is recognition that inflation erodes the value of money. If your interest rate is 10% and the inflation rate is 4%, your real cost of money is only 6%. The loan costs even less if you take advantage of the tax deductibility of mortgage interest. Another advantage to keep in mind is that the value of a property may keep pace with or outpace inflation, while the true value of the amount you owe tends to erode. The opposite is true in a deflationary environment.

28

HOW TO FIND YOUR MARGINAL TAX RATE

In most cases, the interest paid on mortgage loans is deductible from your federal income taxes (see Key 6). You may therefore want to make financing decisions on an after-tax basis, particularly when you are comparing a tax-deductible mortgage loan to a consumer loan. To do so, you need to know your marginal tax rate. This is the amount of each additional dollar of income that is taxed away. It is also the amount of each dollar of tax-deductible expenses that reduces your taxes. So, if you know your marginal tax rate, you can easily determine how much tax you will save.

We can illustrate the use of the marginal tax rate with an example. Suppose a single taxpayer currently rents and is considering buying a home. Her adjusted gross income is $45,000, and she has no itemized deductions. If she buys the home, tax-deductible interest and property taxes would amount to $6,000 the first year. By itemizing, she gives up her standard deduction of $5,150 (based on 2006 tax law), but she would be able to deduct her state income tax payment of $500, so the amount of additional tax deductions would be $1,350. Her marginal tax rate is 25%. Buying the home would save her $337.50 (0.25 times $1,350) in taxes the first year.

To see that this is correct, we can calculate her taxes with and without the additional deductions. As a renter, her taxable income would be $36,550. This is her adjusted gross income of $45,000 less a $3,300 personal exemption and a $5,150 standard deduction; taxes would be $5,809. With the additional deductions, her taxable income is $35,200, and taxes are $5,471. The difference is $338.

In 2006, there are currently six marginal federal tax rates: 10%, 15%, 25%, 28%, 33%, and 35%. You can find the rate for any income range by referring to the Tax Rate Schedules included in the Form 1040 book mailed to most taxpayers in January. You can also find the tax tables and schedules, as well as all the latest information on individual tax returns, in IRS Publication 17 (this document can be downloaded from the IRS Web site at *www.irs.gov/pub/irs-pdf/p17.pdf*).

29

LOAN COMMITMENTS AND LOCK-INS

When you shop for a mortgage loan, you get rate quotes from various lenders and probably pick the lender with one of the lowest interest rates. However, how can you be sure that the loan you eventually get will carry that rate of interest?

The problem is that it takes from four to eight weeks to approve a loan. In today's mortgage market, interest rates can change significantly in that period of time. An increase of one or more percentage points in the interest rate could disqualify you for the loan, in the case of a new purchase, or it could make a refinancing not worthwhile.

Fortunately, most lenders will lock in the rate at loan application. What this means is that the rate quoted when you apply for the loan will be the rate on the loan when approved. The lock-in is good for a specified period of time, generally the amount of time necessary to approve the loan. To get the promised rate, you must close the loan within the lock-in period.

Unfortunately, not all lenders have stood by their lock-in commitments. When interest rates rise rapidly, it is tempting for lenders to renege on the promised rate since making the loan at the original rate will mean an immediate loss for the lender. However, there are key things you can do to minimize the chance of losing a rate commitment:

- Find out whether the lender has a reputation for honoring rate lock-ins and for processing loan applications within a reasonable amount of time.

- Make sure the lock-in guarantee is clearly stated and is in writing as part of the application. Check for any contingencies that would allow the lender to change the rate after application.
- The period of the lock-in should be long enough to allow processing to be completed. For example, a 30-day commitment might be too short. A more reasonable time is 45 or 60 days.
- Be sure to provide all requested information promptly and cooperate with the lender in the processing. This may include making the home accessible to the appraiser when needed.
- Get everything ready to close before the loan is approved. This would include a survey, arranging for inspections, and ordering title insurance.

Suppose interest rates fall during the approval process. You are under no obligation to accept the commitment when offered. You could forfeit your application fee and reapply for a loan at the lower rate. This would delay the closing but might be worthwhile if rates are much lower.

There are loans that allow you to take the locked-in rate or the current market rate, whichever is lower. If you are determined to get the lowest rate possible, or if rates are particularly volatile, you might consider such a loan. However, expect to pay some premium for this service, in the form of either a fee or additional discount points.

For commercial mortgage loans, it is common for lenders to charge a fee for locking in the rate at application. Some home lenders also charge for the lock-in, usually one point. If your best loan option requires a lock-in fee, should you pay it or take your chances on the rate not being changed? If the loan is for a new purchase and a higher rate might mean you can't afford the home, a commitment fee of 1 % might be warranted. On a refinancing, it would probably be better to take your chances, since you can abandon the procedure if things do not work out.

30

LOAN DEFAULT(S) AND FORECLOSURE

Most people who take out mortgage loans repay them with no problems. However, some become unable to keep up the payments, and their loan is foreclosed. It is good to understand default, foreclosure, and the consequences.

When you sign a mortgage note, you promise to repay the loan in a series of monthly payments. You are obligated to make the full amount of these payments every month as contracted. The mortgage pledges the property as security for the lender in case you fail to live up to the requirements of the note. Actually, any violation of the requirements in the mortgage contract is a *default*. However, failure to make payments on time is generally the reason a lender would take action against the borrower.

If you fall behind in your payments, the lender may chose to foreclose the mortgage. The total amount of the loan becomes immediately due. If you fail to pay, the lender can sell the property to satisfy the debt. In some states, this can be done through an official of the local government. The more formal way is to go through the courts in what is called a *judicial foreclosure*. The process can take from three months to a year. In any case, you will end up losing the property.

When the home is sold, the lender (or the mortgage insurer, such as the FHA) may be the successful bidder. However, there will be some method to ensure that a fair price is paid. If this price exceeds the loan amount due plus expenses, you are entitled to the surplus. More realistically, the price will fall short, in which case you may be liable for the deficit. In many states, you can recover the property even after it is sold by satisfying the debt, called *equity of redemption*. It is rare, but possible.

What should you do if you find you can't continue to make the scheduled payments on a mortgage loan?

You might try to sell the property and repay the loan. You will need to get enough for the property to cover the loan and the expenses of the sale (which may be as much as 10% of the sales price). If the loan can be assumed, that may help your chances of a sale. *Beware of offers to take over the loan for a nominal fee.* In economically depressed areas of the country, "con artists" sometimes offer to help people avoid foreclosure by assuming their loans (this is most common with FHA loans) for a fee. The unscrupulous operator takes the fee but never makes any loan payments. The borrower of course, remains liable for the loan.

If you can't sell the home to recover the loan amount, or if you want to try to keep the home, you should discuss the situation with the lender. It may be possible to restructure the loan to delay or reduce payments temporarily. This would be most successful if the problem is a temporary loss of income. In the case of lenders who have sold the loan and are merely collecting payments, the matter may be out of their hands.

The lender may be able to refer you to a debt or foreclosure counseling agency that can help work out a solution. If the lender offers no help, you can find such counseling on your own. Many of the agencies listed at the HUD Web site (*www.hud.gov/offices/hsg/sfh/hcc/ hccprof14.cfm*) also provide such counseling.

You could always walk away from the property and let the lender foreclose. However, there may be some unpleasant consequences in addition to losing your property. You may become liable for any shortfall in the foreclosure sale price. The default may be reported to a credit bureau and prevent you from getting another loan in the future. So, this route should be considered only in the most desperate situations.

31

TAX TREATMENT OF DISCOUNT POINTS PAID

Discount points paid to secure a mortgage loan are deductible from federal income taxes as mortgage interest. However, you may not be able to deduct the entire expense in the year you pay it. The general rule applied by the IRS is that points must be spread over the life of the loan for deduction purposes. An exception to the rule allows you to take the deduction all in one year. To qualify for this favorable exception, all of the following must apply:

- The loan must be for the purpose of buying or improving your principal residence. A second home would not qualify.
- The loan must be secured by your principal residence.
- You must pay the points.
- The charge deducted must be customary for your locality and not include fees for specific services, such as credit reports and appraisals, nor for FHA or VA fees.
- The amount cannot exceed the customary charges in your geographical area.

The list of requirements makes the following fail to qualify for immediate deduction:

- Any loan used to purchase or improve a second home.
- Any loan used to refinance an existing mortgage loan.
- Any second mortgage not used for home improvement.

- Any time you finance the payment of the points.
- Any points paid to buy down the interest rate on the loan.

Your principal residence is the one in which you spend the most time. If you *rent* an apartment in Manhattan and spend five days a week there, even if you *own* a weekend retreat in New Jersey, the rented apartment is your principal residence. The New Jersey place is a second home, even though it is the only home you own. If you have two homes, one in the north for warm-weather use and one in the south for use as a winter residence, the house in which you spend more than half the year is your principal residence. For people who also travel, the calculation can be complex, though the same principles apply.

If your points do not qualify for immediate deduction, you must spread the cost over the life of the loan. For example, if you refinance with a 30-year loan and are charged $3000 for points, you can take a $100 deduction each year you have the loan. If you refinance the home again, any unused deductions can be taken in the year of refinancing, since that expense could no longer be considered prepaid interest. Points paid on the new loan will then be deducted over the life of the new loan.

If you sell the home before you have used up the deductions, the remaining amount can be deducted in the year sold because it could no longer be considered prepaid interest. However, if the buyer assumes the loan, the remaining balance would increase the basis of the property. This will reduce any capital gain you recognize on the sale.

32

FINANCING CLOSING COSTS

Closing costs can add substantially to the cost of financing. Fortunately, some of these costs can be financed into the loan, including discount points and FHA insurance premiums (the MIP). This can reduce your cash needs when making a new purchase or refinancing an existing loan. This may allow you to take advantage of lower interest rates even though you do not have or wish to commit the money required to make the transaction.

When you apply for the loan, ask the lender if you can finance the closing costs and if this changes the terms of the loan. Once you have this information, compare the costs of financing the closing costs to either borrowing the closing costs from an independent source or paying them from savings (see Key 25). Your ability to deduct discount points from your income taxes could be affected by the decision to finance them (see Key 31). To assure the deduction, you need to write a check for the points, so be prepared to pay for the discount points rather than have the amount deducted from the loan proceeds. There will be no difference in the net dollars involved upon loan closing.

You will probably have to finance all of the points and fees or none of them. You will have to qualify under the larger amount of loan, but it cannot exceed the loan-to-value ratio limit set by the lender.

There may be a temptation to try to fool the lender when buying a home, through dual contracts. These are illegal. Using dual contracts, a buyer and seller state the price agreed upon in one contract, but they present a second contract with a fictitious higher price to the lender.

They expect the lender to offer a mortgage based on the higher sales price, so that the loan amount is greater than if the real contract were shown. The effort is to minimize out-of-pocket closing costs for the buyer. However, dual contracts are illegal, so they must be avoided. Furthermore, they may backfire—that is, the seller may try to hold the buyer to the contract with the higher price.

In a refinancing, the appraised value will set the ceiling on the loan amount. If you feel that the appraisal is too low, ask to see it. Perhaps the appraiser missed an important feature of your home, or didn't use, as comparables, sales that you are familiar with. There may be room to increase the loan amount by reviewing the appraisal for a possible increase.

33

REFINANCING WITH FHA AND VA LOANS

You may refinance an FHA or VA loan or use FHA and (if you are eligible) VA loans to refinance a conventional loan. In addition, if you refinance an FHA loan, you may be able to recover some of the prepaid mortgage insurance premium (check with the local FHA office for details).

There are two types of FHA refinancing: streamline and cash-out. Streamline refinancings offer reduced paperwork for homeowners who want to take advantage of lower market interest rates. Cash-out refinancings are for homeowners who want to liquidate some of the equity that has accumulated in their home.

Streamline refinancings require that the loan being retired be FHA insured. The new loan cannot be for more than the remaining balance of the original loan plus the front-end mortgage insurance premium, less any refund of the premium paid at the closing of the original loan. The loan must be current, and the borrower must have a history of timely payment. The refinancing must result in lower monthly principal and interest payments. The borrower cannot use a longer term to reduce the monthly payments—the new loan must have a term no longer than the lesser of 30 years or 12 years beyond the remaining term on the original loan. The original loan must be at least 6 months old. If these conditions are met, the borrower will not have to be approved, and there is no requirement for an appraisal of the property nor a termite inspection. If they cannot be met, you can still refinance with an FHA loan, but you will have to go through at least some of the steps for a new mortgage loan.

You can use an FHA loan to obtain cash from a refinancing, as well. The home must be your residence—no rental property allowed. If the borrower has owned the home at least one year, the new loan is limited to 85% of the current appraised value of the home plus any closing costs that may be financed into the loan. If you have owned the home less than a year, you are limited to 85% of the original purchase price plus closing costs, assuming that this is lower than the current appraised value. This is not a streamline process, and you will have to qualify for the new loan. There may be a new upfront mortgage premium, but you also may receive a refund of part of the premium you paid on the existing loan.

If you have an existing VA loan and want to refinance with a conventional loan, you may be able to get your eligibility reinstated. This will allow you to get another VA loan in the future. You must apply to the VA when the loan is repaid as part of the refinancing. Of course, if you are not a veteran but assumed the VA loan, this doesn't apply.

When you refinance with a VA loan, you can borrow 100% of the value of the home, assuming you have sufficient entitlement to justify that amount of loan.

34

PREPAYMENT PENALTIES

Keys to refinancing include clearing existing loans. One potential impediment is the prepayment penalty on the existing first mortgage. Another is the provisions of the second mortgage, if there is one.

The mortgage contract you sign sets out a method for paying back the loan over the life of the mortgage. The right to pay off the loan early is a privilege that may be in the contract. Some loans, however, require a penalty for this privilege. You may wonder why the lender would want to discourage borrowers from paying back loans early. After all, the sooner the money is repaid, the less risk there is of the borrower defaulting on the loan.

Lenders make loans because they want to receive the specified interest rate over the life of the loan. They know that borrowers will want to refinance loans if interest rates fall. This means that the lender's investment in loans (in their jargon, it is a portfolio of loans) will be replaced with loans at lower rates of interest. Prepayment penalties help to slow down this reduction in the lender's portfolio yield, as well as provide extra income.

The prepayment penalty is set at a specified percentage of the outstanding loan balance. In many cases, this percentage is reduced as the loan matures. For example, the penalty may be 5% of balance for the first year of the loan, 3 % for years 2 and 3, 1% for years 4 and 5, and none afterward.

If the original loan were for $100,000 at 7% interest for 30 years, the balance after one year would be $98,984. The prepayment penalty would be $4,949 under the scale described above. After two years, the balance would be $97,895 and the penalty $2,937 (at 3%). Prepayment from the beginning of year 6 would be free of any penalty.

Fortunately for the borrower, prepayment penalties are becoming increasingly rare. Loans insured by the FHA or guaranteed by the VA do not include such a penalty. Most loans sold into the secondary mortgage market do not provide for a penalty; so your chances of getting a loan without a prepayment penalty are good. If you are refinancing, however, what counts is your existing loan. Before considering prepaying your loan, check to see if your contract stipulates a penalty. It may still be worthwhile to refinance, but you must consider the cost of prepayment in your decision.

Second mortgages can pose serious obstacles to refinancing. Legally, mortgage priority works like this: the first to be recorded is a first lien, the second recorded is a second lien, and so on. When a mortgage is paid off, the mortgages recorded later move up a notch in priority. If you pay off a large first mortgage, the second becomes a first, so you then won't be able to give a first lien. There are two possible solutions: one is for the refinancing amount to be enough to clear all liens. The other is to have a *subordination* clause in the second mortgage, which states that there will always be a first mortgage with priority. The subordination clause will be difficult, if not impossible, to negotiate in a home mortgage.

Prepaying a mortgage is especially advantageous when you have surplus cash available, but cannot find a safe investment opportunity that pays a higher rate than your mortgage. One drawback to this plan is the lack of liquidity, the drain on your cash reserves, that prepayment of a mortgage can cause.

35

SECOND AND VACATION HOMES

Properties other than your principal residence may be refinanced. However, you may be subject to some restrictions on your options and tax deductions. This is particularly true when a second home is not used exclusively by you or your family.

You can finance properties other than your principal residence with an FHA loan. However, the loan-to-value ratio is limited to 85%. If you are refinancing a rental property, you will not be allowed to get a loan for more than the balance of the old loan (you can't get cash out of the property). You must occupy the home to be eligible for a VA loan. However, you can purchase a duplex or other multiple-unit property with a VA loan as long as you occupy one of the units.

For federal income tax purposes, all property taxes on homes you own are deductible. However, mortgage interest is deductible only on your principal residence plus one other home. Your principal residence is the home you spend the most time in and the one used for voter registration and your permanent address. If you are renting an apartment because you moved and could not sell your former residence, you may deduct interest on your former home. You may select any other home you own as your second home, regardless of when you bought it or how much time you occupy the home.

You may have a situation in which you rent out the home a portion of time. If *renters occupy* the home for no more than 14 days of the year, you may consider the home your residence and use the mortgage interest deduction. In addition, you do not need to report the rental income. If *you occupy* the home for 14 days or less, and rent it out the remainder of the year, the property is considered rental property and you cannot deduct any interest as a personal deduction. You can deduct interest, property taxes, and other rental expenses, as well as depreciation, against rental income from the property. If you have more expenses than income, you may take a loss up to $25,000 (but this is reduced if your adjusted gross income, not including losses from the property, exceeds $100,000 and fully eliminated if your adjusted gross income exceeds $150,000).

For situations in which you occupy the home for more than 14 days, but not enough to qualify as a residence, you must allocate your expenses between personal deductions and rental expenses. This is done by dividing the days rented by the number of days in the year and applying the ratio to total expenses on the property. Rental income is reported on Schedule E of Form 1040, and expenses, prorated as described above, are a deductible business expense to be reported on that form. Depreciation can be claimed; however, a second home used in this manner cannot generate a tax loss, even though expenses exceed income.

The remainder of the mortgage interest and property taxes are used as personal deductions. For tax planning, be mindful of the number of days you use the property yourself to maximize your tax deductions.

36

FINDING YOUR HOME'S VALUE

A key to knowing how much you can borrow on your home is to know its market value. Some states restrict the amount of home equity or refinancing to a specific percentage of value. Generally, the higher the percentage you borrow, the higher the interest rate, whether the state restricts the amount or not.

Finding the outstanding debt is easy. You can ask your lender for the amount of your loan balance, or you can calculate it yourself by using a standard table of mortgage amortization rates.

The hard part is finding the value of your home. When you apply for a loan, the lender will have the property appraised to indicate its market value. This is the amount the home would likely sell for in a normal market. The appraised value will set the limit for the loan amount. However, you may want to know this information before committing to the loan.

The most accurate way to find market value is to hire an appraiser. An appraisal should cost about $400. An appraiser is the most qualified person to give you this information, but it may be more accurate than you need for this purpose. Ask your lender which appraisers are acceptable to them, or which professional appraisal designations are acceptable.

Real estate brokers will provide estimates of market value for no charge. However, they will expect that you want to sell the property. You may not want to use the broker if you have no intention of selling.

If you are pretty sure you are going through with the loan, you might get the lender to pre-qualify you. For a nominal fee, the lender will determine how much loan you are eligible for before you commit to a formal application.

If you are willing to do some investigation, you may be able to make a ballpark estimate yourself. For this estimate, you will need some indication of recent sales prices. You may have former neighbors who have sold homes recently. Tell them what you are trying to do and find out the prices they received.

Many lenders have access to automated valuation models (AVMs). These estimate home values using statistical techniques, which are not a substitute for a bona fide appraisal with a personal inspection. Web sites such as *www.zillow.com* may provide some information.

The local property tax district estimates the value of your home, which is public information. However, these estimates are usually unreliable and often well below the true value of the home. Asking prices for similar homes listed in the classified ads may provide some guide. Deduct about 10% from the price and you can get some feel for the current market price of homes like yours. This method may not be very precise, but it will give you an idea of what you have to work with.

Let's say your home is appraised at $250,000. You'll be eligible to borrow 80%, which is $200,000. If you presently owe $140,000, expect to be able to get a $60,000 home equity loan, perhaps reduced by the fees required by the lender.

A detailed explanation of the three approaches to appraisal is provided in the following Key.

37

APPRAISALS

Market Approach. The market data comparison approach is one of the three standard methods for estimating value (appraising). The result is an indication of value based on recent sales of similar properties in the local market. The market approach assumes the typical buyer views the property as an alternative to buying similar property.

The market approach indicator is most reliable when market activity is normal and there are many close substitutes for the property in the market. When activity is slow, it is difficult to obtain enough good comparison sales to derive a reliable indication of value. Also, if the subject property is unusual, there may be no good substitute properties in the market.

To make a market approach value estimate, you must collect information on recent sales of properties similar to your subject property. These sales are called *comparables* or *comps*. The more comparables, the better the analysis, but there should be at least three. The sales prices of the comparables are adjusted to account for any differences between the comparable property and the subject. Adjustments are commonly made for such features as size, physical attributes, condition and quality, date of sale, location, and financing. If special financing was used in the sale, a portion of the sales price may reflect the benefits of the loan to the buyer. In most cases, it is best to avoid use of these comparables. If this is not possible, the price increase due to financing must be purged through a process called *cash equivalence.*

Each adjustment is based on the appraiser's judgment of how much the market is paying for a feature. Adjustments are used to set the price of the comparable at what it would have been if the property had the same features as the subject property. If the comparable is better than the subject, its sales price is adjusted down. If inferior, the comparable's price is adjusted up. After all comparables are adjusted, the appraiser estimates values from among the adjusted sales prices.

The market approach is often the most useful indication when you are interested in what the property will likely sell for in the current market. By looking at the way comparables are adjusted, you may learn how certain features are valued in the market. This may be helpful if you plan to add a feature to or expand the property. The selection of comparables also may indicate how active the market is for properties like yours. If the market is very active, the comparables will be recent. If not, some of them may be six or more months old. The comparables may indicate what features are standard in the market.

Income Approach. The income capitalization approach is one of the three standard methods used to derive value indications. The method is based on the value of the income produced by the property and assumes the typical buyer views the property as an investment. The emphasis is on the financial returns from the property rather than on physical characteristics.

The income approach is most reliable when the property produces current income and is similar to other income-producing properties in the market. The method is not useful to appraise properties held mainly for appreciation or development potential, such as raw land. It is also not used for owner-occupied housing.

However, a variation on the technique, called the *gross rent multiplier*, can be substituted. Comparable sales are taken from the market for rental houses similar to the subject. Gross rent multipliers—sales price divided by monthly gross rent—are calculated for each comparable. A single multiplier is selected to represent the market. It is applied to the subject by estimating what the house would rent for and then multiplying it by the multiplier, as an indication of the property's value.

For income properties, the income approach starts with an estimate of market net operating income (NOI). This figure represents the income the property would produce if leased at rental rates, vacancy rates and operating expenses typical of the market. The NOI is converted into an indication of value by applying a *capitalization rate*. The relationship is:

$$\text{Value} = \frac{\text{Net Operating Income}}{\text{Capitalization Rate}}$$

Capitalization, or cap, rates are taken from recent sales of comparable income properties by dividing their NOI by sales price. This process is similar to the market approach used to derive adjusted sales prices of whole properties or sites. In the absence of good comparables, cap rates may be estimated using various formulas and market data on interest rates and investment returns. Generally, the cap rate is 1 to 2% above the mortgage interest rate for the property, although much depends on the prospects for value appreciation (which justifies a lower cap rate), or expected external depreciation (using a higher cap rate).

Sometimes properties are offered for sale based on a historical cost or replacement cost amount, whereas the income approach would indicate a higher appraised value. These could prove to be excellent buys.

The income approach provides an indication of value in financial investment terms. It can be used to compare the value of the property with that of other types of assets, as well as with other real estate. By using different estimates of NOI, you can see how value might be affected by boosting rents, reducing vacancies, or lowering operating expenses.

Cost Approach. The cost approach is one of the three standard methods for deriving an estimate of value. The approach is based on the cost to reproduce the subject property and assumes the typical buyer considers the option of new construction when viewing the property. The cost approach is often used to support another appraisal approach. However, it may be the primary indication when the property is new, unique, or when market conditions are abnormal.

The cost method generally starts with an estimate of the cost to reproduce an exact replica of the subject property at current rates. This estimate is reduced by the amount of *accrued depreciation* in the subject (see Key 38). This adjustment is necessary because the property is not brand new. (New buildings have little depreciation, so the cost approach is often used to value new construction). The result is an indication of the value of the building alone.

Replacement cost begins with the cost to replace the property, but using modern materials, a modern design, and current construction techniques. Depreciation then is subtracted to derive a value estimate.

The site (land, lot) is valued by using a market approach, as set forth above. These are sales of vacant sites having a use similar to the subject property. The value of the site is added to the building value (cost new minus depreciation) to obtain an indication of property value.

The cost approach might also provide an indication of the value of the building and site separately. It may be useful to estimate how much value is added by the building when a change in use is contemplated. When renovation or modernization is considered, the cost approach may indicate how much value would be added by curing various types of depreciation.

The cost approach is far more appropriate for a new building or proposed new construction than it is for an older property or one with functional or external depreciation. It is best not to rely on the cost approach alone. Cost and value are not the same.

38

DEPRECIATION
IN VALUE

Some people believe that real estate only increases in value. It is true that inflation together with the forces of supply and demand tend to cause real estate values to rise. (Of course, falling demand and oversupply can cause values to fall, as well). In addition, age causes deterioration of manmade parts of a property, and that decreases value over time. In most cases, appreciation can be credited to the land value because of the advantages a particular location provides the property. Often, increases in land value exceed the decline in structure value. The proof of this is when the structure no longer has value and is removed for new construction.

When buying real estate, try to determine how much depreciation the property has suffered and whether it can or should be repaired or rehabilitated, and then estimate the remaining useful life of the property. In a number of instances, a small improvement in a deteriorated property results in a handsome return on investment. In other cases, the needed repairs are so extensive that they are not worth doing. The key to *curability* is whether the repair outlay will be returned through higher rents or value enhancement.

Another consideration is whether the property should be bought as it is. The price may be low enough to make the property attractive despite the depreciation sustained and lack of curability.

There are three main sources of depreciation in real estate value: physical, functional, and external. Physical depreciation is the result of deterioration of the structure with age. Part of this is due to normal wear and tear. Nothing lasts forever and each year the structure is closer to the time when it will no longer be useful. Components of the structure break or wear out periodically and must be replaced. Physical depreciation can be slowed by a good maintenance program. In fact, certain types of depreciation, such as faded paint, are referred to as "deferred maintenance." However, a point may be reached when the building is so old that continued maintenance and repair is not feasible.

Functional depreciation, or *obsolescence*, refers to the design or style of the building. Technological advances and changes in tastes are reflected in new construction. Since a building lasts for a relatively long time, it increasingly represents the technology and style of the past. In some examples, this is good, in that it may give the building historic character and appeal to nostalgia. In many instances, the building is merely outdated, inefficient, and no longer commands top prices. Functional depreciation can be offset to some extent by remodeling and modernization.

The third source of depreciation is external, meaning depreciation caused by outside forces. A noisy or traffic-generating property may have been built next to a quiet residential street, causing a decline in housing values. There is little the property owner can do to cure external depreciation.

39

LUMP-SUM SECOND MORTGAGES

Second mortgages are often used to finance a down payment for a home purchase, but they can also be used to refinance a home. In fact, even if you currently have a second mortgage on your home, you may still be able to use this method. The new loan could be used to refinance the second loan or added on in the form of a third mortgage.* It all depends on whether you have sufficient value in your home to justify increased debt (see Key 36).

You may consider a lump sum second mortgage in these two instances:

First, when you want to keep the first mortgage in effect. This may be to avoid a prepayment penalty (Key 34) or because the existing mortgage has a low interest rate (Key 26). If you don't want to keep the existing mortgage, consider refinancing with a new first mortgage.

Second, when the cash you need is for immediate use and you don't anticipate future borrowing. For example, you may need the money to pay a large medical bill, make property improvements, or buy additional property. If you think you will need additional financing in the future, such as to pay for a child's college tuition over a four-year period, you should consider a line of credit home equity mortgage (Key 40).

You apply for a second mortgage just as you would for a first mortgage. The lender will have the home appraised and the value will determine how much you can borrow. You probably will be limited to some frac-

---

*In this book, *second mortgage* refers to any financing added to that used to buy the home. *Junior mortgage* is a broader term that applies to any lien below the first mortgage.

tion of the home's value to provide adequate security for the loan. Second mortgages usually carry higher rates of interest and shorter terms than first mortgage loans. This is because the lender is not in as good a legal position to enforce the claim in case you default (a third mortgage provides weaker protection than a second, and so on).

After getting the loan, you pay it back in monthly payments of interest and principal. You can calculate these payments just as you did for a first mortgage. As an example, suppose you own a house valued at $250,000. Your existing mortgage has a balance of $170,000, leaving you with $80,000 in equity. You can decide to borrow $40,000 of that over 10 years. The second mortgage will be at 7% interest for ten years. Monthly payments on the second mortgage are $464.43. This is in addition to the payments you currently make for the existing mortgage.

The good news about second mortgages is that the interest you pay is deductible from your taxable income. However, there is a limit of $100,000 on the amount of debt over the balance of the existing purchase loan, and the loans combined cannot exceed the market value of your home. The bad news is that you must pledge your home as security for the loan. This means you may lose your home if you can't pay the loan back (even if you keep up the payments on your old mortgage loan). You should be especially prudent when considering a second mortgage loan.

40

HOME EQUITY LINES OF CREDIT AND REVOLVING PLANS

A home equity line of credit is set up like a second mortgage loan (see Key 39), but the borrower does not have to draw all of the money out of the loan at one time. This type of loan is well-suited for:

- Borrowers who anticipate that they will need more money in the near future, but do not need it immediately. For instance, you may plan to use the money to start a business and anticipate losing money for the first few years. Another application might be for college tuition, in which you expect to draw upon the loan for each semester's expenses.
- Refinancing credit card balances and other consumer credit accounts. The home equity line can function much like the consumer loan, yet interest is still tax deductible.

Setting up a home equity line can be as simple as applying for a credit card. However, since you are giving a second mortgage on your home, there will be some processing involved, including an appraisal of the property. The application fee necessary to pay for all this may be 1 to 2% of the line of credit for which you are applying. There has been intensive competition among lenders to originate home equity loans, so you may find lenders willing to reduce or even waive this fee. Some plans also charge an annual fee to encourage the borrower to use the line once it has been granted. In addition, many plans require that you take out a minimum amount when the loan is granted.

Many home equity lines have variable interest rates pegged to some index of interest rates. This means your payments may vary over time. Furthermore, the rate may be changed frequently, perhaps every month or whenever the index changes. Few loans offer *caps*, or limits, on how much the interest rate can change over a specified period of time. This feature tends to make the loans a bit risky for the borrower.

There are a variety of ways to repay the loans. Some require fixed payments similar to lump-sum mortgage loans. Others allow the borrower to pay as much as he or she wants each month. This is similar to the way most credit cards operate. A few offer payment plans where you pay only interest for several years before paying back any of the principal. Many lenders, particularly commercial banks, offer automatic debiting from your checking account to cover the payments.

Home equity lines of credit offer a flexible way to access your home equity, thereby financing periodic needs with tax-deductible interest. You may tailor the plan to the way you want to handle the payments. You can draw upon the line with checks (good for infrequent, large withdrawals) or credit card (for frequent, smaller withdrawals).

41

HOME EQUITY LOAN HAZARDS

Although often used as consumer credit programs, home equity loans are serious financial obligations. A key is to remember that your home is pledged as security for a loan, and failing to meet your obligation could result in losing it.

Don't be misled by flexible repayment plans. Many people get into financial difficulties because they cannot control their use of credit cards. It is tempting to pay the minimum and let the balance pile up. It is wise to keep your balance at a point where you could pay off the loan by selling other assets, if need be. This way, you are taking advantage of the liquidity and tax features of the loan without jeopardizing your home.

If the interest rate on the loan rises, try to accelerate your payments. If the loan does not have caps on rate adjustments, you may want to refinance with a loan that does.

Loans with interest-only payments or first-year teaser rates can be deceptive. Base your decision to take the loan on the full payment scheduled later in the term. It's okay to take advantage of these offers as long as you can fit the higher payments into your budget later on.

If your loan requires a lump-sum payment in the future, have some realistic plan for making this payment. Either identify a source for the money or get a written refinancing agreement with the loan.

Whenever you borrow on equity, you are more vulnerable to the value of your home declining. This is a real possibility no matter what part of the country you live in. If you owe more than your home is worth, it can actually cost you money to sell the home. You may end up trapped in your present home.

If you are applying for a line of credit, be prudent in how much you ask for. The line should be related to some definite need. Any closing costs associated with the loan will be based on the amount of the line, not what you actually use. There may be an annual fee to encourage you to use the line granted.

Before you go the home equity route, check on the cost of alternative types of financing. Even though home equity loans enjoy a tax advantage, remember that the tax break is in the form of itemized deductions. If you don't have enough deductions from other sources (mortgage interest on your existing home loan, property and local income taxes, etc.) at least equal to the standard deduction, some of the tax advantage is offset. You may even recalculate last year's taxes with and without the loan to decide on how much you will save.

A difficulty may arise when you have a second mortgage or home equity loan and you want to refinance your first mortgage. If the first mortgage is retired, the second mortgage automatically moves to first priority. This will inhibit a potential first mortgage lender from lending. So, even though you just want to replace a high-interest rate first mortgage with another first mortgage of the same principal, this may be prevented by your second mortgage.

All of these caveats take on a special urgency when total debt exceeds the value of the property. The so-called "125%" mortgage makes this situation a real possibility for those who accept this type of financing. When the value of the home is more than the debt outstanding, you can always sell the home and pay off the loans with the proceeds (though you may have to eat the cost of selling the home). But when the debt is more, this possibility is precluded and if you cannot make the payments, the only alternative is to give up the home. This might appear okay on the surface, except that home lenders today are more diligent in pursuing deficiency judgments following foreclosure. This means that after you lose the home, you still may not be out of the woods. The lender can sue for any losses incurred in recovering the principal and interest due on the loan. Such an experience could make it difficult to reestablish your good credit rating in the future.

Borrowing all of the money that is offered to you has been likened to eating *all* of the food at a restaurant buffet. It will make you ill. Remember that money borrowed must be repaid eventually. It is not income. In the case of a home equity loan, failure to make payments may do more than damage your credit rating; it may lead to your losing the house.

42

HOME EQUITY LOAN SOURCES

A key to finding the right loan is to consider all available sources. Traditional second mortgage lenders are described in Key 10. The emergence of home equity programs has enlarged the field of lenders. Likely lenders are among the following:

- **Banks.** Commercial banks are attracted to home equity lines as a way to sell other bank services, such as savings accounts and credit cards. Banks have been some of the most aggressive marketers of home equity loans, offering low closing costs, special initial interest rates, and no annual fees. If you open an account with the bank, you may be able to automatically debit the account for payments on the loan.
- **Consumer Finance Companies.** These firms have long experience in making second mortgages on homes. They have also been aggressive home equity loan makers in an effort to keep borrowers who want to retain tax-deductible interest.
- **Savings and Loan Associations.** The S&Ls have moved into home equity more cautiously. However, these loans are natural extensions of their first mortgage business.
- **Mortgage Bankers.** These lenders do not retain the loans they make but sell them in what is called the secondary market. As home equity loans become more acceptable to investors and other purchasers of mortgage loans, mortgage bankers can be expected to offer more programs.

- **Credit Unions.** These organizations should provide equity loans for the same reasons as consumer finance companies.
- **Securities Brokerage Firms.** Stockbrokers are more than just securities salespeople. Many of the major companies offer their own line or sell programs offered by the large investment houses. They may offer to margin securities you own, or lend more provided your purpose is not to buy more securities. Ask for a "nonpurpose" loan.
- **Nontraditional Lenders.** A major university provides student loans backed by home equity. Some home improvements dealers also offer equity financing for these products and services.
- **Online Lenders.** Many mortgage banking companies have an Internet presence, as well as their bricks-and-mortar offices, while others operate through Web sites only. Though the latter are not chartered banks, they do have to comply with all federal lending laws.

With home equity loans, you often do not have to search out sources. If you own a home and have a good credit rating, the lenders will seek you out.

43

CONVERTING NONDEDUCTIBLE INTEREST

The tax deduction for personal interest was eliminated in 1991. However, the deduction for mortgage interest remains. Moreover, you can take out a mortgage loan in excess of your current debt and use the money for any purpose, including the retirement of consumer debt. Provided the additional loan is $100,000 or less, and your home is worth more than all loans on it, all interest is deductible as housing interest.

The tax advantages of mortgage credit have encouraged a growing number of homeowners to convert their consumer loans to mortgage debt using home equity loans. Consumer purposes include auto, education, boat, signature, and bank loans, as well as store credit programs and credit cards.

To decide what loans you should convert, follow these steps:

1. Find out how much you owe on each loan and what the interest rate is.
2. Find out how much your home is worth.
3. Get quotes on available home equity loans and calculate the after-tax interest rate.
4. Compare the cost of converting the loans, one by one.

An example illustrates the process. Suppose you have the following debts:

Car loan	$4000 at 9%
College loan	$5000 at 3% (subsidized low interest)
Credit card #1	$1000 at 15%
Credit card #2	$2500 at 8%

Your home is worth $250,000 and the mortgage loan has a balance of $170,000. You can borrow up to about $75,000 on a home equity loan. You call some home equity lenders and find a loan offered at 7%. Your marginal tax rate is 28%. By itemizing interest payments, you save 28 cents in taxes for each dollar of additional interest you pay. Therefore, your after-tax cost is 72 cents per dollar. For the home equity loan, that makes the after-tax interest rate only 5% (.72 times 7%).

You should definitely pay off the car loan and the balance on credit card number one (and tear it up). The college loan is still a good deal even if no interest is deductible. You also decide to pay off the balance on credit card number two, but keep the card for travel expenses and convenience. To retire all three loans (but not the college loan), you need a home equity loan of $7500 (or you might establish a line of credit of $30,000, keeping some reserve for future expenditures). The amount needed is well below the limit set by your available home equity.

44

USING YOUR HOME TO FINANCE INVESTMENTS

It may seem curious for someone to borrow money to invest. Generally, investing is something you do with money you don't currently need. However, there are two key reasons why you might consider investing money you don't have. First, you may be able to take advantage of *leverage*. That is, you hope to increase your investment return by reducing the amount of cash you have to put into the investment. Leverage only works when the return you expect to make from the investment is greater than the cost of the borrowed money. This is how banks make money. They invest money at a return higher than the rate they are paying on it. The second reason is *diversification*. By borrowing, you may be able to spread your money among a variety of investments, thereby protecting yourself from disappointment in a few ventures. Some investments, such as real estate, require such large chunks of money that the only reasonable way to invest is through borrowing.

By using home equity credit, you may be able to reduce the cost of investment borrowing and make leverage work in your favor, or you may be able to increase the scale of your investments. Consider the following possibilities:

- Home equity might be less expensive than the interest charged by brokers when buying stock on margin. In addition, you don't face margin calls if the price of the stock goes down.

- You might be able to use home equity to borrow the down payment on a piece of real estate. This may allow you to buy additional properties or a larger property than if you only mortgaged the properties.

You may be able to take advantage of an assumable loan on a piece of real estate. Often, when a loan is assumable, the required cash investment is large. The combination of the assumed loan and home equity financing may be less expensive than all-new financing.

Ordinarily, interest on borrowed money would be nondeductible if you own tax-free municipal bonds. But you can buy municipal bonds and still deduct the interest expense of financing your home.

You can borrow on home equity to purchase shares in a partnership. Passive loss restrictions in the tax law prevent you from charging off losses greater than the income from the partnership. However, if you use home equity to finance your purchase, you can deduct the interest even if the partnership produces no taxable income.

Keep in mind the cautions of using home equity financing. It makes little sense to put your home in jeopardy to finance highly risky or speculative investments.

45

INCREASING YOUR DEDUCTIBLE INTEREST

Under current tax law, a homeowner may be subject to different limitations on deductible mortgage interest, depending on when he or she took out a second mortgage or refinanced a mortgage.

All mortgages taken out before October 13, 1987 are eligible for itemized interest deduction. This debt, whether first or second mortgage, provides fully deductible interest, provided the debt does not exceed the fair market value of the home as of October 13, 1987. The fair market value is presumed to be at least as much as the purchase price plus the cost of improvements. If you had a mortgage before October 13, 1987, and refinanced it after then, interest on the same principal as the old loan is fully deductible. But to the extent that the new principal exceeds the old amount, interest may be limited.

Loans taken out after October 13, 1987, fit into two categories: those to buy, build, or substantially improve your home and those not to buy, build, or substantially improve.

For loans to buy, build, or substantially improve your home, interest on up to $1 million of debt (including pre-October 1987 debt borrowed for one of those purposes) may be deducted. The ceiling is $500,000 for married persons who file separate tax returns. This type of debt is called *acquisition debt.*

Up to two homes can be used for acquisition debt, the one in which you live as a main home and one other.

You must live in the other at least 14 days a year. If it is rented out part of the year, your personal use must exceed 10% of the number of days it was rented at a fair rental. To be eligible, the second home must have basic living accommodations, including sleeping, cooking, and toilet facilities.

Mortgages for any other purpose are called *home equity mortgages*. Housing interest includes home equity mortgages up to $100,000 ($50,000 for married taxpayers who file separate returns). There is no qualification on how you use the money.

When a home equity mortgage exceeds the limit, it is considered a mixed-use mortgage. A pro rata share of it generates tax-deductible housing interest, and the rest is personal interest.

For example, in September 2000 you refinanced your home for $250,000. It was worth at least that much at that time. You may continue to deduct all of the interest. The same would be allowed for a very expensive home.

Another example. In January 2006 you bought a home for $250,000. Later that year you spent another $150,000 in capital improvements to substantially improve it. You can borrow up to $500,000 in tax-deductible housing interest: $400,000 is treated as acquisition debt and $100,000 is home equity debt. However, the house must be worth at least $500,000 to do so.

46

MORTGAGES FOR RETIREMENT INCOME

Young households often find it difficult to buy their first house. Older retired households generally experience the opposite situation. Their housing is taken care of—indeed, most people over 65 own their home outright—but they need cash income. They are "house rich and cash poor."

They could sell the home, but they would have to move, and most would find this undesirable. However, there are ways to convert some of their equity into income without moving.

The Home Equity Conversion Mortgage (HECM) is FHA's version of the *reverse mortgage*. A traditional mortgage loan provides a lump sum now and is paid back over time. The reverse mortgage provides money over time and is paid back later, usually when the home is sold. Reverse mortgages were introduced in the early 1980s, but high interest rates made them impractical. The HECM was begun in 1989 by the FHA. The loan itself is made by private mortgage lenders, with FHA insuring the lender against loss. (There are reverse mortgages not insured by FHA, but they are a small part of the market.)

To apply for an HECM, you must be at least 62 years old and own your home free and clear (or have a very small remaining debt). Closing costs and the FHA premium are paid out of loan proceeds. Interest on the loan is taken out of monthly draws on the loan, with the borrower getting the remainder in monthly payments. When the loan becomes due or you move from the home, the loan is paid off by selling the home.

There are several different options for receiving payments. You may set the loan up as a tenure annuity. This provides income for as long as you live in the home. This option generally provides the lowest level of income, but you don't have to worry about being forced to move from the home. The monthly income is based on the life expectancy of you or your spouse, whichever is longer. The older you are when the loan starts, the greater the monthly income. Second, you may set up a term annuity of various lengths. This provides income for a specified period of time. The longer the term, the smaller the monthly income becomes. Third, you may choose to establish a line of credit that you can draw upon as needed. The term of the loan depends on how much you use the line of credit.

The FHA has a model (see *www.reverse.org*) to determine how much income you could derive from each option. The amount depends on your age, the mortgage interest rate (which can be fixed or adjustable), and the value of your equity in the home. Counseling is provided to help you choose the appropriate option for your situation.

As an example of the difference in options, suppose a retired home owner applies for an HECM. The homeowner is 75 years old and owns free and clear a home worth $200,000. The mortgage interest rate is fixed at 10%. Closing costs and FHA premium are $3500. A tenure annuity based on the homeowner's life expectancy would provide an income of $744 per month for as long as the homeowner lives in the home. The homeowner could instead take a lump sum of $116,260 at closing.

Credit counseling may be required as a condition of loan approval. If you are considering a reverse mortgage, get a copy of the booklet "Homemade Money," published by AARP (*www.aarp.org/money/report/*).

47

REFINANCING TO REDUCE INTEREST COSTS

If you are a borrower with a fixed-rate mortgage loan, you have a key advantage. You can decide when to refinance. If interest rates go up, you are unaffected, as the interest rate on the loan is unchanged. If the loan is assumable and you sell the home, you may actually gain in the form of a higher sales price. By contrast, if interest rates go down, you can refinance the loan and take advantage of the lower rates.

Mortgage interest rates can vary substantially over time. In mid-1982, the national average interest rate on fixed-rate home loans was over 15.5%. By the early 2000s, the average rate had dropped to about 6%. This amount of change can make a big difference in your loan payments.

For example, suppose you took out a home loan in 1982 for $80,000 at 15%. For a 30-year loan, your monthly payments for principal and interest would have been $1011.56. In 1992, you found you could refinance the loan at 8% interest. If you refinanced the outstanding balance of the old loan, your monthly payments would decline to $563.68 on a new 30-year loan. This is a reduction in payment amount of 44%. To keep the remaining term at 20 years, the payment would become $642.56, a 36% savings.

Of course, it does cost money to refinance the loan (see Key 24). In general, it is worth considering refinancing when the current interest rate is one or more percentage points below the rate on your loan (see Key 48 for a more detailed analysis).

One difficulty, however, lies in selecting the best moment to refinance—when interest rates bottom. This is never known in advance. You need to refinance at some point when it is favorable. If interest rates decline further, you can refinance again. Although you will incur transaction costs twice, it will be better than missing each opportunity. A reversal of the interest rate trend can occur sharply and suddenly, and you will regret failing to take advantage of the earlier decline.

Some homeowners play a game: they apply for a loan and accept a 45- or 60-day lock-in, offered without cost. During the lock-in period, they watch interest rates. If rates decline, they apply again; if rates rise, they claim the locked-in rate, which is now substantially below the market. However, this strategy can backfire because lenders have ways of avoiding loan commitments when rates suddenly reverse (see Key 29).

A "float-down" commitment allows the borrower to take advantage of a reduction in rates without having to start the loan process from scratch. At closing, the borrower has the option of taking the locked-in rate or the current rate, whichever is lower. For that privilege, the borrower pays a extra commitment fee. The borrower can invoke this choice anytime during the loan approval process, but when it is invoked, the commitment converts to a standard lock. In general, a float-down commitment should cost about one discount point more than a standard lock of comparable length.

Finally, refinancing a first mortgage can be hampered when there is a second mortgage. The second will automatically move to top priority the instant the first mortgage is retired, thus inhibiting a new first mortgage. Often, the only way to get a new first mortgage is to retire all liens on the property.

48

WHEN YOU SHOULD REFINANCE

When interest rates decline, you can save money on your home loan by refinancing with a new loan. However, refinancing costs money. Therefore, you must decide if the savings are enough to justify the costs of refinancing.

This problem is not difficult if you think of the refinancing as an investment. You are investing the costs of getting a new loan and receiving reduced monthly payments in return. The monthly savings continue until you retire the new loan. Therefore, you need to estimate how long you will have to keep the loan (and the home) to recover your investment. Beyond that time, the savings are a pure return on your investment.

Here are the steps required for this type of analysis:

1. Get information on the loans currently available. This includes the interest rate, number of points, and term.
2. Find out the current balance on your loan. You may ask the lender for this information.
3. Find out if you have to pay a prepayment penalty on your current loan. If so, calculate how much the penalty will be.
4. Add up the costs of refinancing. This includes the prepayment penalty, the application fee for the new loan, and all closing costs on the new loan. Ask the lender you have chosen for an estimate of these closing costs. This estimate need not be precise, but should be a good approximation of the costs.

5. Calculate the payments on the new loan. You can do this using a table or find out from the lender.
6. Calculate the after-tax payments of both your current loan and new loan. You may just multiply the monthly principal and interest payment (subtract out the escrow) by one minus your marginal tax rate (see Key 28). This is close enough for this analysis. Now subtract the new payment from the old payment to find the monthly savings.
7. Compare the savings to the costs to find the amount of time before you break even. This can be done several ways:
   a. *Payback method.* Simply divide the costs by the savings. This gives you the number of months required to recover your investment.
   b. *Discount method.* The payback method assumes that money in the future is worth as much as money now (see Key 27). A more realistic method uses a discount rate. This is the interest rate you could earn on money you invest. Estimate the rate (what can you earn from a bank CD) and the money you could earn each month. Use the monthly savings as the payment and the costs as the loan amount and find the term of the loan. This is your break-even period.

If you finance all closing costs into the loan, you can simply look at the monthly savings. Since the refinancing does not involve a cash outlay, this savings is your return for refinancing (refer to the tables in Key 29).

Here's an example. The current loan has an interest rate of 10%, a balance of $98,837, and 26 years left to run. The monthly payment is $890.50. There is a prepayment penalty of 2% of the balance ($1,977). The new loan is at 7% for 30 years and requires one discount point. To refinance the outstanding balance of the old loan, the payments will be $657.56.

The borrower's marginal tax rate is 28%, so that the after-tax cost of the old loan is $641.16 (890.5 times 0.72

the cost) and the new loan cost is $473.44. The savings is $167.72 per month. Costs of refinancing are as follows:

Prepayment	$1,977
Points	988
Application	300
Appraisal, survey, other	500
Total costs	$3,765

With the payback method, it will take 22.5 months to recover the costs ($3,765 divided by $167). At a discount rate of 6%, it will take 24 months to recover. Therefore, if the borrower plans to stay in the home for more than two years, it pays to refinance the loan. If the closing costs are financed into the loan, the new loan will be $102,602 (the balance of the old loan plus the closing costs). The monthly payment will be $682.61, giving a monthly savings of $149 per month after taxes. Although the principal balance is increased and the mortgage term is lengthened, the monthly payment savings in two years more than offsets the costs.

Only principal and interest payments are relevant for these calculations. Property taxes and insurance will be the same no matter how the property is financed.

49

RETIRING A
HOME MORTGAGE

Few mortgage loans run to their full amortization term. Instead, they are retired early through sale of the home or refinancing. An old rule of thumb was that the average life of a loan was 12 years. However, the actual average depends on how frequently people move and changes in interest rates. When rates move upward, people tend to hold onto their loans, but when rates drop, many refinance to take advantage of the lower rates.

The chances are that you will retire your home loan before it matures. In most cases, you will replace the loan with a new one on your existing home. If you sell and the buyer assumes the loan and later defaults, the lender can look to either you or the current owner to cure the default or pay any deficiency if foreclosed. If you pay the lender, you can look to your buyer for repayment. If instead of assuming, the buyer takes the property *subject to* the loan, the buyer does not accept mortgage liability. In this case, you remain solely obligated for the loan. If the buyer defaults, the lender looks to you to make the loan good, and you have no one to look to. In a default, often the recent owner has moved away or has no money. The bottom line: when you sell a home with the existing financing, *get released from the loan if possible.* Get the new owner to substitute for you. The document that accomplishes this has a fancy name: **novation**. Enlist the help of a lawyer or title company to get released from the loan.

Although some people say they wouldn't mind getting their old property back upon default, defaults seldom occur when there is much equity in the property. The property may be run down, the mortgage many months in arrears, or the area economically depressed when the default occurs. Avoid mortgage liability whenever you can.

When no assumption is involved, you will retire the old loan and open the new one in a simultaneous transaction. To retire the old loan, you will need to pay the outstanding principal balance, any accrued interest, and a prepayment penalty, if applied, less the accumulation in your escrow account. This money will come from the proceeds of the new loan. Any excess can be used for your down payment on the new home or taken out in cash. The proceeds of refinancing are not taxable income. You should get a release document, called a *satisfaction piece or satisfaction of mortgage*, from the lender showing that you are no longer liable for the debt. This document should be recorded at the courthouse to clear the title to the property.

If you are concerned about the amount of interest you pay over the life of a loan, you may reduce the amount by partially retiring the principal. Many lenders allow you to make additional payments toward the principal along with your regular payment. This won't reduce your monthly payment, but will shorten the maturity of the loan.

50

WHEN TO CONSIDER PAYING OFF A LOAN EARLY

You may not have thought of it as such, but paying off a mortgage in cash is a refinancing decision. In this case, you are replacing your mortgage debt with equity. For most people, this is only possible when the loan is very old and most of the balance has been paid down. In other words, retiring the loan is possible only when the balance is small enough that you have the money to pay it off.

Let's look at the conditions under which it may be wise to pay off the loan. Your first consideration should be **liquidity**. You don't want to use money that you have set aside for emergencies or have earmarked for some future need. It wouldn't make sense to retire a loan costing 7% interest and then have to borrow money at 12% interest. Think of paying off the loan as an investment in an illiquid asset.

Secondly, consider the **savings possible**. The money used to pay off the loan could be earning interest. The interest you could earn should be less than the interest rate on the mortgage. If not, it will not pay to retire the loan. Are you itemizing the mortgage interest on your tax return? If the loan is old, you may not have enough interest to itemize. If you don't itemize, reduce the interest rate you could earn on the money by your marginal tax rate to make the comparison.

At times, lenders offer discounts as an inducement for borrowers with old mortgages to pay them off. The interest they are earning from the loan is much lower than they could earn on new loans, so they are anxious to get rid of old loans. You can analyze this decision by thinking of the payoff as an investment of the balance of the loan minus the amount of the discount. The IRS considers the discount as income (forgiveness of a debt is taxable income), so you will have to add in the amount of tax on the discount. Your return for making this investment is the remaining monthly payments you will not have to make. Compare this rate to what you could make on the money if invested.

Here's an example. Suppose you have five years remaining on a mortgage loan at 7% interest. The balance is $20,000. You have this amount in maturing bank CDs paying 8.5%. Should you use this money to pay off the loan? Your marginal tax rate is 15% and you don't itemize. The return from the CDs is 7.25% after taxes, so you are still better off leaving the money in the bank.

Now, suppose the lender offers to discount the loan balance by 10% if you pay it off. This reduces the $20,000 balance by $2,000, but you will pay taxes of $300 on the discount. The net amount needed to pay off the loan is $18,300 ($20,000 minus $2,000 plus $300). Your monthly payments are $396. You search through a mortgage table to find a match of five years of payments at $396 per month and a loan amount of $18,300. The interest rate is between 10.75% and 11 %. This is more than you can earn by investing the money safely, so you make the logical decision and use the money to retire the loan.

51

PAYING DOWN YOUR LOAN

You can save a significant amount of interest on your loan by reducing the time to pay it off. The reason that mortgage loans have long terms (often 25 or 30 years) is to stretch out the cost so as to reduce the monthly payment. However, a main drawback of a long-term loan is that the interest paid over the life of the loan may be some three or more times the amount actually borrowed.

There are a number of types of loans that provide rapid amortization. The easiest to arrange is a 15-year mortgage. This will significantly increase each and every principal and interest (P&I) payment, typically by 20%. A bi-weekly mortgage is another approach. The payment required is one half of a monthly payment for a standard mortgage. This amount is paid every two weeks. Because there are 26 two-week periods in a year, it is similar to making 13 monthly payments in a year. However, such payments will significantly shorten the amortization period, although they may adversely affect affordability, especially if you are stretching the budget to buy the home. It is especially useful, though, for people who are paid every week or every two weeks, but not for those paid monthly or even twice a month (which is not quite the same as every two weeks).

An alternative is to arrange a 30-year loan to keep the payments at an affordable level. Then, you can pay more each month or in a lump sum when you have some extra cash. Keep this important caveat in mind: if you encounter hardship after making extra payments, your lender may not be amenable to reducing or skipping your future payments. You must still pay regularly.

Before prepaying part of a loan, be certain that your lender will cooperate by applying the extra payment to the current principal balance. Some lenders apply prepayments to the escrow account or to the last required payments—unfavorable procedures for a borrower. Fortunately, some lenders make it easy to apply advance payments to the principal by providing a space on the coupon book so you can indicate the application of an extra payment. It works like this: the principal and interest (P&I) portion of your payment (don't count taxes and interest) has been financially engineered to pay off (or *amortize*, a fancy word for loan reduction) the loan over a certain period, with interest due on the unpaid balance. In a long-term mortgage loan, most of the payments in the early years are for interest, with a small amount for principal reduction (amortization). As the loan is reduced, less of the P&I payment goes for interest and more is used to reduce the debt. Suppose you make an extra payment to reduce the principal. Thereafter, future interest will be less, so more of the payment will reduce the principal, and hasten the reduction of the debt. Any advance payment effectively earns compound interest at the same rate as the mortgage bears, and the advance payment, plus earnings based on it, will shorten the loan term.

Upon making an extra payment, you might want to know exactly how long the new term will be. You can use the following tables to figure this out. However, you will need to know the current principal balance, P&I payment, and loan interest rate.

First, multiply your P&I payment by 1,000. Next, divide that by the new principal balance after prepayment (current outstanding balance minus the extra amount you will pay) to result in a factor. Match that number, as closely as possible, to the table column under your interest rate.

Here's an example. You now owe $80,000 on a 7% rate mortgage with a 20-year remaining term. Your monthly P&I payment is $620.24. You just received a bonus of $2,500 and want to apply all of it to your loan principal. The additional payment will immediately reduce the principal balance to $77,500. Now, multiply your regular monthly P&I payment by 1,000; this is $620,240. Divide by your new principal of $77,500 to equal 8.0031. Look at the following table to find that number under your 7% interest rate column. In the column, you note 7.9419 at 19 years, which gives a good approximation of the new remaining term (it is actually 18 years plus eight months). You will have shortened your mortgage's life by about 16 months. By reducing a mortgage, you will earn at the mortgage interest rate.

If, on the other hand, you placed the $2,500 bonus in a savings account that earned tax-free interest at 4%, with monthly compounding, it would grow to $5,286 in 18 years, 8 months. This is not enough to retire the mortgage balance then. The balance will be $9,448 in 18 years, 8 months.

Also note that if interest rates have declined since you arranged your mortgage, you may get much better results by refinancing the entire loan than you would by paying it down faster.

Table for Finding Remaining Term of Loan

Remaining Term (Years)	INTEREST RATE 7.00	7.50	8.00	8.50	9.00
5	19.8012	20.0379	20.2764	20.5165	20.7584
6	17.0490	17.2901	17.5332	17.7784	18.0255
7	15.0927	15.3383	15.5862	15.8365	16.0891
8	13.6337	13.8839	14.1367	14.3921	14.6502
9	12.5063	12.7610	13.0187	13.2794	13.5429
10	11.6108	11.8702	12.1328	12.3986	12.6676
11	10.8841	11.1480	11.4154	11.6864	11.9608
12	10.2838	10.5523	10.8245	11.1006	11.3803
13	9.7807	10.0537	10.3307	10.6118	10.8968
14	9.3540	9.6314	9.9132	10.1992	10.4894
15	8.9883	9.2701	9.5565	9.8474	10.1427
16	8.6721	8.9583	9.2493	9.5449	9.8452
17	8.3966	8.6871	8.9826	9.2829	9.5880
18	8.1550	8.4497	8.7496	9.0546	9.3644

19	7.9419	8.2408	8.5450	8.8545	9.1690
20	7.7530	8.0559	8.3644	8.6782	8.9973
21	7.5847	7.8917	8.2043	8.5224	8.8458
22	7.4342	7.7451	8.0618	8.3841	8.7117
23	7.2992	7.6139	7.9345	8.2609	8.5927
24	7.1776	7.4960	7.8205	8.1508	8.4866
25	7.0678	7.3899	7.7182	8.0523	8.3920
26	6.9684	7.2941	7.6260	7.9638	8.3072
27	6.8781	7.2073	7.5428	7.8842	8.2313
28	6.7961	7.1287	7.4676	7.8125	8.1630
29	6.7213	7.0572	7.3995	7.7477	8.1016
30	6.6530	6.9921	7.3376	7.6891	8.0462

Remaining Term (Years)	INTEREST RATE				
	9.50	10.00	10.50	11.00	11.50
5	21.0019	21.2470	21.4939	21.7424	21.9926
6	18.2747	18.5258	18.7790	19.0341	19.2912
7	16.3440	16.6012	16.8607	17.1224	17.3865
8	14.9109	15.1742	15.4400	15.7084	15.9794
9	13.8094	14.0787	14.3509	14.6259	14.9037
10	12.9398	13.2151	13.4935	13.7750	14.0595
11	12.2386	12.5199	12.8045	13.0923	13.3835
12	11.6637	11.9508	12.2414	12.5356	12.8332
13	11.1857	11.4785	11.7750	12.0753	12.3792
14	10.7837	11.0820	11.3843	11.6905	12.0006
15	10.4422	10.7461	11.0540	11.3660	11.6819
16	10.1499	10.4590	10.7724	11.0900	11.4116
17	9.8978	10.2121	10.5308	10.8538	11.1810
18	9.6791	9.9984	10.3223	10.6505	10.9830
19	9.4884	9.8126	10.1414	10.4746	10.8122
20	9.3213	9.6502	9.9838	10.3219	10.6643
21	9.1743	9.5078	9.8460	10.1887	10.5358
22	9.0446	9.3825	9.7251	10.0722	10.4237
23	8.9297	9.2718	9.6187	9.9701	10.3258
24	8.8277	9.1739	9.5248	9.8803	10.2400
25	8.7370	9.0870	9.4418	9.8011	10.1647
26	8.6560	9.0098	9.3683	9.7313	10.0984
27	8.5836	8.9410	9.3030	9.6695	10.0401
28	8.5188	8.8796	9.2450	9.6148	9.9886
29	8.4607	8.8248	9.1934	9.5663	9.9431
30	8.4085	8.7757	9.1474	9.5232	9.9029

52

REFINANCING UNDER FINANCIAL DISTRESS

Suppose you were able to qualify for a home mortgage only because you and your spouse work. You need both paychecks to afford the loan payments. However, one of you loses the job and suddenly you are left with only one income. Your shrunken budget is not enough for the payment and other necessities. You may try to sell the home, but the market is soft and you can't get enough out to cover the mortgage amount. Do you abandon the home and default on the loan?

This may not be your only option. You may be able to restructure the loan so that you can afford it. At least you may be able to buy time until your income is reinstated. Here are a few considerations:

- **Extend the maturity.** You may be able to negotiate an extension to the maturity of the loan. If the loan is relatively new, this has very limited effect. Most lenders can't extend the maturity beyond 30 years. In addition, the extension of a few years will have a small effect on payments. For example, the monthly payment on a 25-year, 7% interest loan of $150,000 is $1,060.17. If the loan were extended to 30 years, the payment would be reduced to $997.95.

- **Pay only interest.** A more promising option is to temporarily pay interest only. You pay only the interest due on the principal balance and do not retire any of the balance. When you start making principal payments again, the monthly payment will be higher than before unless the maturity of the loan is also extended. In the example above, payment of only interest would reduce payments to $875 per month.

- **Arrange for negative amortization.** If the interest payment alone is too high, you might be able to restructure the loan to require some payment below the interest due. This would be set at the maximum amount you could afford and would be for some limited period. During the time of reduced payments, the balance of the loan will be increasing since the difference between your payment and the interest due is added to the principal. In our example loan, if you pay $800 a month, $75 would be added to principal in the first month. This amount would gradually increase since the principal balance and the interest due increases.
- **Refinance at a lower rate of interest.** If interest rates have declined since you took out the loan, you can refinance at the lower rate. See Key 47 for more details.

When it becomes apparent that you cannot make the loan payments, contact the lender. You will want to avoid having the lender start foreclosure proceedings against you. Once the lender forecloses, the entire loan becomes due, not just the lapsed monthly payments. The lender would like to avoid foreclosure and forced sale of the house and may be willing to work out a loan restructuring. If you can get a co-signer on the loan, it may help the negotiation.

Some loans, going by various names, such as "flexible," "smart," or "option" mortgages, allow you to alter the amount you pay each month. At any time during the life of the loan, you may convert the loan to interest-only, make a minimum payment (somewhat like a credit card), or even skip a payment. Of course, any time you fail to pay at least enough to cover the interest accrued, you create negative amortization, and your debt actually becomes larger with each payment. This type of loan can be helpful for someone with variable income, but you need the discipline to make up for missed interest payments when the cash is available.

53

REFINANCING SHORT-TERM LOANS

Sometimes refinancing is not done by choice, but out of necessity. You must arrange new financing because your existing financing is expiring and there is a balance due. There are several situations where you may have temporary financing:

- You had the home newly built and still have a construction loan or a bridge loan extending beyond the term of the construction loan. These types of loans carry higher interest rates than regular home loans. You will want to find "permanent 'financing as soon as possible (a permanent loan is the long-term financing for the period you own the home).

- When you bought the home, the seller provided the financing as an inducement to make a sale. Often, loans of this type are set up with monthly payments based on a long-term schedule. However, after a few years, the entire outstanding balance becomes due as a "balloon payment." For example, a loan might be for $50,000 at 10% interest with payments according to a 30-year schedule. Monthly payments are $438.79. After the third year, the balance of $49,075.82 becomes due.

The reason a seller sets up the loan this way is to limit his or her exposure to the risks of a lender. A buyer might be attracted to the arrangement because the loan is made at a rate of interest lower than the prevailing rate, or the buyer can't qualify for a loan from a lending institution. If you have one of these loans, you should consider the term of the loan as an opportunity to arrange permanent financing.

Suppose the balloon payment is coming due and you can't find permanent financing. You may be able to negotiate with the seller to extend the loan. If not, you may have to sell the home.

There are other types of loans used to attract buyers that may present refinancing opportunities. When interest rates are high, builders sometimes offer "buy-down" loans. These loans provide a below-market interest rate for the first several years of the loan term. The rate may even be graduated. For example, the interest rate may start at 9% the first year and rise to 10% the second and so on until it reaches the market rate. These are not adjustable-rate mortgages. The schedule of rate increases is fixed. However, if interest rates decline, you may find you can refinance with a fixed-rate loan at a lower rate. This is a standard refinancing as described in Key 47.

Another type of loan that is similar to the buy-down is a "graduated-payment mortgage." In this, the interest rate is fixed, but the payments are reduced for the first few years. This means the principal balance actually increases during those years. You may still refinance (base your decision on whether there is a lower interest rate available on new financing), but the amount of the new loan may need to be more than the original one.

54

HOW ARMS DIFFER FROM FIXED-RATE LOANS

Adjustable-rate mortgages (ARMs) are an innovation of the 1980s. Today, they are offered by virtually all mortgage lenders and are an important part of the market. There is one major difference between ARMs and fixed-rate mortgages: the interest rate on a fixed-rate mortgage does not change over the entire life of the loan. This means that the monthly payment of principal and interest is never changed (your monthly payment may vary due to changes in the escrow payment for taxes and insurance, which changes independent of interest rates). In contrast, the interest rate on an ARM may be adjusted from time to time, meaning that your principal and interest payment may vary from one year to the next.

The interest rate on an ARM is related to an index specified by the lender (see Key 57). This index tends to rise and fall as interest rates change in the economy. Most ARMs are set up to be adjusted once a year on the anniversary date of the origination of the loan. If, when the time comes to adjust the rate, the index has gone up, the lender will raise the interest rate applied to the loan. If the index has fallen, the rate is adjusted downward. The difference between the value of the index and the interest rate on the loan is called the "margin." This margin does not change over the life of the loan. The interest rate is adjusted periodically to maintain this constant margin versus the index. The effect is similar to refinancing the loan balance at each anniversary date with a new interest rate.

An ARM has several advantages and disadvantages compared to a fixed-rate loan. One advantage is that most ARMs are initially offered at interest rates below those on fixed-rate loans. This means you may save money at least during the first year of the loan. It also may mean that you can qualify to borrow more than if you selected a fixed-rate loan (although this is harder to do if you are borrowing 90% or more of the purchase price). Another advantage is that you get automatic, free refinancing when interest rates fall. The main disadvantage, however, is that your monthly payments may increase if interest rates rise. The problem of increased payments is limited by the use of adjustment caps (see Key 55), although the amount of potential increase is still substantial.

Here is an example to show how ARMs work and how they differ from fixed-rate mortgages. Suppose you had bought a home at the end of 2006 and took out a loan for $200,000. You may have taken a fixed-rate loan at an interest rate of 6%, for example. Alternatively, you could have used an ARM originated at 4%, which you considered a great bargain. The ARM's interest rate is not fixed, but pegged to an index that reflects the yield on one-year securities issued by the federal government. Suppose that, at the time of origination, this index had a value of 1.3%, so that the margin on the ARM is 2.7 percentage points (4 minus 1.3 equals 2.7). This margin will be reestablished each year when the ARM rate is adjusted.

Let's run through the first several years of the loan to see how the interest rate changes and the effect it has on the monthly payments, especially in relation to the fixed-rate loan, which requires the same payment each year. The first table shows the index value, the ARM interest rate, and the monthly payment on the ARM. For reference, the fixed-rate mortgage interest rate is 6%, and the monthly principal and interest payment is $1,199.10 (both alternative loans are amortized over 30 years).

Year	Index	Margin	ARM Interest Rate	ARM Payment
1	1.3%	2.7	4%	$954.83
2	2.7%	2.7	5.375%*	$1,115.59
3	4.4%	2.7	7%	$1,315.58
4	4.0%	2.7	6.625%	$1,269.17
5	2.5%	2.7	5.125%	$1,095.41

*Rates are commonly rounded to the nearest eighth of a percentage point when adjusted.

In this case, you were a bit unlucky if you chose the ARM, since interest rates rose dramatically in the years after you got the loan. In fact, that bargain ARM turned costly in year 3 when your payment actually exceeded that on the fixed-rate loan. However, rates did fall almost as steeply in the next few years, so that the payment fell back to a level lower than that of the fixed-rate loan. Note how the original 2.7 percentage rate margin between index and interest rate was maintained except for the slight distortion caused by rounding.

In the example above, there are no restrictions on how the ARM rate is adjusted. The interest rate is changed to whatever the index plus margin equals, no matter how volatile the index. Large changes in an index number can lead to big swings in the interest rate and payment increases that can cause problems for ARM borrowers. That is why many ARMs feature adjustment caps. Let us see how our example might work out if annual adjustments to the ARM interest rate are limited by a one-percentage-point annual cap.

Year	Index	ARM Interest Rate	ARM Payment
1	1.3%	4%	$954.83
2	2.7%	5%	$1,070.52
3	4.4%	6%	$1,189.54
4	4.0%	6.625%	$1,264.97
5	2.5%	5.625%	$1,148.17

The adjustment after the first year is restricted to the one percentage point allowed by the cap, so the rate is 5% in year 2 instead of to the 5.375% allowed in the unrestricted ARM. The effect of the cap results in a monthly saving of $45 in year 2. The cap comes into play once again in the third year, so that the rate is a full percentage point lower than the unrestricted ARM. The effect of the cap results in a monthly savings of $125 in year 3. Keep in mind that the ARM rate should be equal to the index value plus margin, except that, if that requires an increase greater than the cap allows, the rate increase (or decrease) is limited by the cap. In year 4, the full 2.7% margin is reestablished since the adjustment required is less than the cap. However, this means that the interest rate and payment increased despite the fact that the index declined slightly. On top of that, the payment exceeded that of the fixed-rate loan (which you didn't select in 2006). The index fell further in year 5, but the cap, which operates on the down side as well (not all caps do this, so find out when loan shopping), limited the effect of the decline. The borrower of the capped ARM ironically ends up with a higher payment in year 5 compared to the unrestricted ARM.

Some very popular ARMs have a fixed interest rate for several years in the beginning of the loan term, then turn into one-year adjustable ARMs. These loans may have caps applied to the adjustable period.

Selecting an ARM is more complex than negotiating fixed-rate loans and introduces a new type of risk for the borrower. However, these mortgages offer the opportunity to save money on interest payments if interest rates do not increase substantially.

An important factor in selecting an ARM or a fixed-rate loan is the volatility of interest rates. Generally, in a period of high volatility, you want the predictability of a fixed rate. Also important is the slope of the yield curve. A positive slope (which is the normal situation) means that the rate on short-term borrowings is less than for long-term borrowings. When this is the case, the ARM will provide reduced payments compared to the fixed-rate loan—until there is a general increase in interest rates.

55

ADJUSTABLE-RATE MORTGAGE TERMS

Adjustable-rate mortgages (ARMS) are long-term mortgage loans with variable interest rates. They have a schedule of principal and interest payments just like a fixed-rate mortgage, but the interest rate may be adjusted at regular intervals during the term of the loan. Therefore, the monthly payments are likely to move up and down as the rate is adjusted (some ARMs have variable terms, so that the monthly payment may stay the same, but the maturity of the loan changes).

An ARM is an important financing alternative for first and second mortgages. In addition, many home equity loans are structured as ARMS.

In addition to the contract interest rate, discount points, loan-to-value ratio, and maturity, ARMs have their own unique set of terms:

- **Adjustment Interval.** Most ARMs are adjusted at regular intervals stated in the mortgage contract. In between these intervals, the interest rate on the loan is constant. The shorter the interval, the more sensitive the loan is to changing interest rates. Most first mortgage ARMs are adjusted annually. Some are adjusted every six months. Second mortgages may be adjusted more frequently. Some allow the lender to change the interest rate without changing the payment amount. If the interest rate is raised, the principal of the loan may increase, a process called *negative amortization*.
- **Initial Interest Rate.** All ARMs have an interest rate that is fixed until the first adjustment date. Sometimes this rate is set low to attract borrowers

and called a *teaser rate*. Therefore, the initial interest rate does not indicate the long-term cost of the loan. The future interest rate is dependent on the index and margin.

- **Index.** All ARMs use an index to peg the direction and amount of adjustment in the interest rate. The index is some economic indicator that is related to interest rates in the market (see Key 57).
- **Margin.** There may be a margin that represents the difference between the index value and the interest rate that could be charged on the loan. Suppose the current interest rate on an ARM is 6%. At the time of adjustment, the index sits at 4%. If the margin is three percentage points, the interest rate could be increased to 7% (the index plus the margin).
- **Caps.** Many ARMs offer a sort of insurance against large adjustments in the interest rate in the form of caps. There are two types of caps. An annual adjustment cap limits the amount of change that can be made at one time. Therefore, if the cap is two percentage points, the interest rate cannot rise more than that amount, regardless of how much change occurs in the index. Caps may apply to decreases as well as increases. The second type of cap limits the total amount of change during the life of the loan. If an ARM is originated with a rate of 6% and has a lifetime cap of five percentage points, the rate can never be higher than 11%.
- **Convertibility.** Some ARMs provide the borrower with the option to convert to a fixed-rate loan during the loan term. See Key 58 for more details.

The various ways that loan payments can be arranged provide for a menu of ARM loans tailored to fit a wide array of concerns. Here are two of the more popular alternatives to a standard ARM:

- **Hybrid ARM.** The interest rate on this type of loan is fixed for the first several years, then adjusted annually until the end of the term. Such loans go by self-explanatory names. Thus, a 5/1 ARM is fixed for the first 5 years and adjusts annually starting in year 6. Other hybrids are 3/1, 7/1, and 10/1. The loans are priced somewhere between fixed-rate and annually adjusted ARMs. They appeal to borrowers who think they may have difficulty qualifying at the market rate on fixed-rate loans, as well as those who see a good probability of refinancing or selling the home by the end of the fixed-rate period.

- **Option ARM.** These loans are also called "flexible-payment" loans. The borrower can select payment options that fully amortize the principal (like a standard mortgage loan), cover only the interest accrued, or, for temporary intervals, negatively amortize. Reduced payments create negative amortization (a condition where the loan principal grows) by allowing the borrower to skip a payment, and some provide for a minimum payment, similar to a credit card. The borrower may pay exactly the interest amount or more to amortize over 15 or 30 years. These loans are suited for homebuyers with variable income or those who anticipate large expenses that interrupt their ability to make loan payments. They should be taken out only by borrowers with the financial discipline to handle the additional financial risk inherent in the use of negative amortization.

Option ARM loan programs could be right for you if you expect to own your property for only a short time and prefer affordability and flexibility in your monthly payment. However, if you select a reduced payment option in the early years, you should be prepared for possible sudden increases in your monthly payments thereafter. The borrower must understand that there is no free lunch. A reduced payment will cause a payment increase later, plus compound interest.

56

EVALUATING AN ADJUSTABLE-RATE MORTGAGE

Although the interest rate on an ARM may start out relatively low, it can rise above the rates on fixed-rate loans over time. This is the major concern of borrowers considering an ARM. Therefore, when deciding on a loan, evaluate the risk of rising payments.

It is not possible to forecast interest rates with any degree of reliability. Instead of trying to figure out if rates are going up, you should calculate what the loan payments will do if rates do rise. In this way, you can tell how much impact such a rise in payments would have on your family budget and ability to make your payments.

To do this, you need to know how an ARM works so that you can simulate the effect of interest rate changes on monthly payments (see *Barron's Adjustable Rate Mortgages* for a complete guide). To simulate an adjustment to the loan interest rate:

1. Calculate the balance on the loan. If the loan is adjusted annually, you can use a mortgage amortization table. If adjusted more frequently, you will have to do a month-by-month calculation. For each month, multiply the old balance by the interest rate divided by 12 to get the interest paid. Subtract this amount from the principal and interest payment to obtain the principal reduction. Then subtract this amount from the old balance to get the new balance.

2. Calculate the new payment and, using a table, find the new interest rate. The term will be the original term minus the year of the adjustment. The new payment is indicated in the table.

Here's an example of a simulation. Suppose an ARM starts out with an interest rate of 7%. The balance is $100,000 and the term is 30 years. The ARM is adjusted annually. If the index rises by one percentage point per year, what will the monthly payments be?

Year	Interest Rate	Principal and Interest	Balance at End of Year	Monthly Income to Cover Payment
1	7%	$665.30	$98,984.19	$2,661
2	8%	732.43	98,081.14	2,930
3	9%	800.64	97,267.80	3,203
4	10%	869.67	96,525.12	3,479

The last column is the income needed to keep the payment at 25% of total income. This is one way to evaluate how the increased payments would impact your budget. If your income rose by the indicated amount, the payment increase would not represent an increased burden. Keep in mind, however, that interest rates may change by either more or less than shown above. Also, if the ARM has caps, they may limit rate changes.

A sample of first-year payments for the first 12 months on various types of loans might look like this, per $100,000 borrowed:

30-year fixed-rate at 6.5%
$632.06

5/1 hybrid at 6%
$600.00

1-year ARM at 5.5%
$567.79

57

ADJUSTABLE-RATE MORTGAGE INDEXES

Since the index determines how the interest rate is changed, it is important to the behavior of an adjustable-rate loan. In general, indexes are related to interest rates in the market. However, some interest rates tend to be more volatile than others; from the other point of view, some indexes are more stable. Indexes based on short-term rates tend to be more volatile than those based on long-term rates.

A loan indexed to a long-term rate has less chance of large adjustments than one tied to a short-term index. However, lenders tend to use an index that matches the adjustment interval. For example, a loan that adjusts annually will probably be indexed to one-year security rates.

A variety of indexes have been used with ARMS. A good index should be based on a series that you can verify with public information (published in the newspaper or available from a government agency) and be beyond the control of the lender (usually, some national or regional average). Some of the more commonly used indexes are:

- *National average interest rate on new mortgages.* This is a long-term rate and may be based on mortgages used to purchase either newly built or used houses. Use of this index makes the loan act as if you refinanced it at the going rate at each adjustment interval.
- *Average cost of funds.* This is the average rate paid by lenders for the money they use to make loans,

including deposits, CDs, and borrowed money. It is basically a short-term index, but is less sensitive than most other short-term indexes.

- *Treasury yields.* The U.S. Treasury is constantly issuing securities to fund government expenditures. These securities are issued in a variety of maturities, and the index is based on the market yields that investors receive from the current issue of a specified maturity. Most commonly used is the yield on one-year securities. Therefore, this is a short-term index and can be very sensitive to market change.
- *Bank prime rate.* This is the rate that banks charge their best customers. It is a short-term rate since it is applied to short-term loans. However, it is less sensitive than most other short-term interest rates. The prime rate is used extensively for home equity loans.
- *LIBOR (London Interbank Offered Rate).* This rate is determined by the activities of banks participating in the London money market. The rate appeals to mortgage investors in the global market, an increasingly important source of funds for home loans in the United States. The rate is adjusted daily and therefore provides a potentially volatile index when interest rates are moving.

The Federal Home Loan Bank Board publishes a report that lists past values of various APM indexes. You might find a copy of this list to compare indexes based on their historic behavior.

The weekly financial newspaper, *Barron's,* publishes current index rates for adjustable-rate mortgages. You can check the index value to determine whether you are being charged the right rate when the index changes.

58

CONVERTIBLE ADJUSTABLE-RATE MORTGAGES

Borrowers are attracted to adjustable-rate mortgages (ARMs) because their initial interest rates are often much lower than those on fixed-rate mortgages. However, there is a very good chance that the rate will rise over the life of the loan, and that makes many borrowers leery. Therefore, at some point, you may want to refinance your ARM with a fixed-rate mortgage to lock in the rate for the future. However, refinancing can be expensive (see Key 24).

The alternative is to get a convertible ARM. A convertible ARM gives you the right to convert the loan to a fixed rate during some specified period of the loan term. The conversion involves a fee, but is much less expensive and time-consuming than refinancing. Because the processing is short, you don't run the risk of losing a rate lock-in because of delays (see Key 29). However, unlike refinancing, you can't convert for a higher loan balance and take some equity out in the form of cash.

If you are shopping for a home loan and think a convertible ARM would be appealing, check the following features:

- *Price of the convertible feature.* If a convertible ARM is offered at the same terms as a regular ARM, there is no reason not to take it. However, the lender may require a higher initial interest rate, additional points, or a larger margin over the index as compensation for allowing the convertibility option. The convertible feature may still be worthwhile if you are concerned about the possibility of interest rates rising.

- *Window period.* Most loans allow conversion only during a specified period, often through the second to fifth year of the loan.
- *Conversion fee.* If you convert, a nominal fee may be charged. It could be a flat fee of several hundred dollars or a percentage of the loan balance. The fee should be much lower than the cost of refinancing.
- *Rate on converted loan.* The fixed-rate loan that you will get upon conversion will be at the prevailing rate at the time of conversion plus a premium. This premium is usually some fraction of a percentage point.

If you have a convertible ARM, you face the decision of when you should exercise the option. Often, borrowers are pressured to convert when interest rates are going up since they are fearful of higher monthly payments. However, this may be the wrong time to convert. For example, suppose your convertible ARM had an initial rate of 5%, an adjustment cap of two percentage points, and a lifetime cap of five percentage points. You can convert to a fixed-rate loan at .5 percentage point above the going rate. In the second year of the loan, your ARM is adjusted to a rate of 7%. The fixed loan rate is 8.5%, so you could convert to a 9% fixed-rate loan. However, if you don't convert, your ARM can rise only as high as 10% (5% plus 5% cap) and may come down as interest rates ease.

A better time for conversion is when interest rates are coming down. Suppose the example ARM above was adjusted to 4% in the second year and fixed rates fell to 6%. You can convert to a fixed-rate loan at 6.5% and be protected against future increases, which could reach as high as 10%.

59

HOME IMPROVEMENT FINANCING OPTIONS

Most home owners eventually find it necessary to remodel, repair, or make additions to their homes. These projects can cost several thousands of dollars and often require some type of financing. Going into debt to improve your home can be a good investment since the work may increase the value of your home.

Whether a home improvement adds to value depends on how it appeals to the likely buyer for the home. The most valuable improvements are those that bring the home up to the standards of other homes in the neighborhood or price range. In general, these will add to the convenience and attractiveness of the home. Custom features that appeal to your specific needs and tastes may not be fully appreciated by the next buyer. Some improvements represent an "overimprovement," a feature that would not normally be found in homes in your price range. In most cases, the value of your home is bounded by the surrounding homes. A luxury home in an area of starter homes will not garner a significantly higher price. Some improvements, such as swimming pools and converted garages, may even be a detriment to resale. If you do not plan to move soon and desire such features, it may still be worthwhile to make the improvement. You should be aware that you may not recover your investment when you sell the home.

There are several ways to finance improvements. One option is to refinance your existing mortgage with a new first lien mortgage. You will probably be limited to converting a portion of accumulated equity to finance the improvements. Therefore, the value of the home should be enough to cover the old loan amount, the cost of the improvements, and the margin of equity required by the new loan. For example, if your home will be worth $100,000 after the home improvements are made, and the mortgage balance is now $60,000, you could finance $20,000 worth of improvements with a new 80% mortgage.

A second alternative is a second mortgage from a traditional mortgage lender (see Key 10). The same limitation applies here as for a new first mortgage. However, you may not want to disturb the existing mortgage because of a favorable rate or to save refinancing expenses. With some of these loans, you can write checks to pay the contractor as improvements are made, up to the specified line-of-credit limit. You need not use the full line of credit if you don't want to.

When shopping for a second mortgage, inquire about FHA Title I loans. These loans are offered for home improvements and mobile home purchases and may provide better terms than a conventional second mortgage.

The home improvement contractor may be another source of financing. This type of financing may be easier to arrange than a loan from a mortgage lender. However, convenience may have a price, so compare the terms with those from an outside source before committing. If the project is relatively small or you are acting as your own contractor, you may finance the job with unsecured credit. This may be credit from the materials supplier or a bank loan. The terms of the loan may not be as good as a mortgage loan and you will not be able to fully deduct interest payments from your income taxes. Fortunately, you won't incur the closing costs generally required to take out a mortgage loan.

60

TAX CONSIDERATIONS ON A HOME IMPROVEMENT LOAN

- **Deductibility of interest on home improvement loan.** If you used a mortgage to finance the improvements, you may deduct all interest paid on the loan during the year, except for loans beyond $1 million. For a second mortgage or home equity loan, you are subject to the limits discussed in Key 6. If the loan is not secured by a mortgage on your home, deductibility is limited or prevented because it is considered to be personal interest.
- **Deductibility of points paid on a home improvement loan.** Points are deductible, but must be spread over the term of the loan (see Key 31). The amount you may deduct in each year is equal to the cost of the points divided by the number of years in the loan term.
- **Adjusting the basis of your home.** The amount you spend for improvements is added to the tax basis of your home. Add the cost of the improvements to your original purchase cost (don't include the costs of interest on the loan). Adjusting your basis is important if you own a high-priced home and may have to pay taxes on resale profits.

61

TAX PROBLEMS
AT RESALE

If you sell your home for more than you paid for it, you may owe taxes on the sale. Gains from the sale of a home are taxable income. Fortunately, tax law allows a generous exemption on this gain if you have lived in the home for several years. However, there are cases where the real estate market does not allow a sale.

In general, the gain from sale of a home is calculated as the difference between the net selling price and the adjusted basis of the home. The net selling price is the price you received for the home minus expenses of sale. The adjusted basis is what you originally paid for the home (including brokerage commissions and fees you paid) plus the amount spent for any capital improvements (long-lasting additions) made to the home. If you have lived in the home as your principal residence for three of the previous five years, you can exempt up to $500,000 ($250,000 for single or separately filing taxpayers) of realized gains from taxation.

This exemption means that, for most people, the sale of a home is tax-free. Even if the gains are above the $500,000/$250,000 limit (not too far-fetched in cases where profits from previous home sales are reflected in the basis of the home sold), the exemption serves to greatly reduce the taxes owed. However, problems may occur when circumstances prevent the home owner from qualifying because of the residency requirement.

Suppose you need to sell your current home because you are transferring to another part of the country. There is no market for the home when you need to sell. Not wanting to leave the home vacant, you decide to rent it out until the market improves. The slump drags on and you continue to rent. It is possible to violate the three-year rule and lose the right to an exemption. When the home is sold, it will be subject to a tax on the full capital gain to be reported on Schedule D of Form 1040.

Very active markets may also present a problem. Suppose you sell your home and take advantage of the exemption. A year later, you are offered a very high price for your new home. You take advantage of the opportunity to sell and improve your housing. You will not be able to take an exemption on the second sale because the tax laws allow only one exemption within a two-year interval.

62

ASSUMABLE LOANS AND RESALE VALUE

If you have a mortgage loan that can be assumed by a buyer, it may add to the price you can get for the home. The value of an assumable loan comes from two sources. It is often easier for the buyer to qualify when assuming a loan and the payments may be lower than for new financing. However, its value may be limited by two important factors. If the balance of the loan is much below the asking price, the loan may not be worth much. For the buyer to assume, either a large cash down payment is required or additional financing will be needed. This extra financing may be a loan provided by the seller. Second, if the rate on the existing loan is close to or above the going rate, there is little advantage to assuming it.

How do you know if your loan is assumable? An FHA or VA loan is likely to be assumable. A conventional loan is not likely to be assumable. Look in your loan contract for a "due on sale" clause. If it is there, the lender has the right to call in the loan when you sell the home. There are assumable conventional loans that require a slightly higher interest rate.

If you have an assumable loan at an interest rate below the market, you should get a higher price at the sale. Remember that when you repurchase, you will have to pay more for financing. A higher resale price compensates you for giving up favorable financing.

How much is the loan worth? Consider that since the loan payments are lower, the buyer could pay a higher price and still make the same payments. Say you have a home that is worth $200,000. You have an assumable loan for $140,000 at 6% interest. There are 25 years left in the term. A new loan for $140,000 at the prevailing rate of 8% and 30 years requires a monthly payment of $1,027.27. Your loan's payments are $902.02. The monthly savings of $125.25 would service a loan at the market rate over 25 years for $16,228. Therefore, a buyer who assumes the loan could borrow an additional $16,000 and still enjoy lower payments than by using totally new financing. Whether you could extract this amount in the sales price depends on market conditions. However, the assumable loan provides an important sales tool in any market.

If you think you may sell your home in the near future, you may want to refinance with a new assumable loan at a relatively high loan-to-value ratio. This will provide a form of insurance in case interest rates rise or mortgages become hard to obtain when you do sell.

63

PROCEEDS FROM RESALE

The sale of your home can be a refinancing decision since you will be changing the financing. In most cases, when you sell, you will have proceeds—the difference between the net sales price of the home and the balance of your old mortgage loan. The refinancing decision involves how to invest these proceeds.

You will probably be buying a home to replace the one you sold. Therefore, some of the proceeds will be required for a down payment on the new home. You could put all the proceeds in to buy a more expensive home or to minimize your mortgage payments. Alternatively, you could take out some of the equity to spend or invest. You may want to buy the new home with an assumable, high loan-to-value ratio loan to make the next resale easier (see Key 62). The decision revolves around the cost of the mortgage loan versus other borrowing or investment opportunities.

As an example, suppose you sold a home for $300,000 and retired the old loan of $160,000. Ignoring other costs, you have $140,000 in resale proceeds. You decide to buy a new home for $320,000. If you invest the entire proceeds in the home, the loan will be for $180,000. At 8% interest, 30-year term, your monthly payments would be $1,320.77. On the other hand, if you take out a loan for 80% of the cost, the loan will be $256,000 and monthly payments are $1,878.44. This second alternative provides you with $76,000 in cash after making the down payment on the home.

Which alternative should you take? Consider the following:

- Can you invest the remaining proceeds to yield more than the cost of the loan?
- Do you have enough ready funds to handle emergencies? If not, you may want to retain some proceeds to provide this cushion, no matter what you give up in relative costs.
- Do you have some necessary expenditure, such as medical or education expenses? By using the proceeds for these purposes, you may avoid borrowing at a higher cost. Home equity loans will probably cost more than the first mortgage. Consumer credit is not only more expensive, but the interest is not tax deductible. By contrast, the 8% rate on the mortgage loan is 5% after-tax to taxpayers in the 33% bracket.
- How do the higher monthly payments on the larger loan fit into your monthly budget? In the example, the difference in payments is more than $557 per month. If you don't have a good use for the money, it may be better to invest it in the home and reduce your financial burden.

QUESTIONS AND ANSWERS

How does a mortgage loan differ from other types of loans?

A mortgage loan is a secured loan. When you get the loan, you pledge a property to the lender to back up your promise to repay the debt. Personal loans are generally backed only by the borrower's signature and past credit history. Because these loans are thus unsecured, the interest rates tend to be high. Since real estate tends to hold its value better than other durables, such as automobiles and boats, a home is a valuable security for a lender. That is why the lender is willing to lend you a large amount of money at a relatively low interest rate.

Most mortgage loans are long-term loans and are self-amortizing. This means that the regular loan payments include a portion to pay back the loan principal over the term of the loan.

Is it better to get the largest loan you can or to make the largest down payment you can?

The standard mortgage loan covers 80% of the cost of the home. However, mortgage loans are made for amounts ranging from less than 50% up to as much as 97.5% of cost. Most people who get high loan-to-value loans do so because they don't have much cash. Even if you have more money, you may not want to put it all in the home purchase. Once invested, it may be difficult to get the money out if you need cash in an emergency. If you buy a home as an investment, a larger loan gives you more leverage. Your profits from appreciation will be a higher percentage of your equity. On the other hand, a larger loan will require higher monthly payments. If your income declines, you may have difficulty meeting this obligation. In addition, loans with a high loan-to-value ratio may require a higher rate of interest and additional expenses for mortgage insurance.

How does a mortgage loan affect my income taxes?

All interest paid on a mortgage loan used to purchase a home is an itemized deduction for federal income taxes, up to a limit of $1 million in loan principal. For a second mortgage or refinanced first mortgage, interest is deductible up to a limit of $ 100,000 over the amount of the loan used to purchase the home. These deductions apply to both first and second homes, and the property value must exceed the debts.

What is the difference between a first and second mortgage?

A first mortgage gives the lender first claim to the home in the case of default on the loan. After the loan is foreclosed and the home is sold to satisfy the debt of the first mortgage, any sales proceeds left can be claimed by the holder of the second mortgage. Because of this priority, a first mortgage is less risky for the lender than a second mortgage. Consequently, interest rates and terms on first mortgage loans are more favorable to the borrower. In most cases, second mortgage loans are used to take equity out of the home when it is desirable to preserve the existing first mortgage loan.

What is the purpose of mortgage insurance?

Mortgage lenders consider a loan of 80% of the value of the home the maximum amount of risk exposure they may undertake. However, they will make loans for higher amounts if the loan is insured against borrower default. The Federal Housing Administration (FHA) offers mortgage insurance on loans below a specified dollar amount. Larger loans may be insured by private companies specializing in this service. In addition, the Department of Veterans Affairs guarantees loans for eligible military veterans. The guarantee is not the same as insurance, but it has the effect of allowing the borrower to get a loan with a very small down payment.

What should I know about discount points?

Discount points are charged by mortgage lenders as part of the cost of getting a loan. Each point is equal to 1% of the loan amount. In most cases, the charge is not for any particular service, but is additional interest on the loan. Therefore, points add to the effective interest rate on the loan. Points on loans to buy a house may be deductible as mortgage interest from your taxable income, provided certain conditions are met. In refinancing, the deduction for points must be spread out over the life of the loan.

Why are some people turned down when they apply for a loan?

Before lenders grant mortgage loans, they assess the risk that the borrower will default on the payments. This is called "qualifying the borrower" and depends heavily on a credit score based on the credit history of the applicant. People are generally turned down if they don't have established credit, if they have had a loan foreclosed in the past, if their income is too low to support the payment burden, or if their existing debt is too high to allow for additional debt. Certain qualifying standards must be met for the loan to be approved for FHA insurance or VA guarantees. Even those granting conventional loans use relatively standard qualifying procedures in order to make those loans acceptable in the secondary market.

How expensive is it to refinance a mortgage?

Fees for refinancing may be more expensive than for the original loan. If you are replacing an existing loan, you may have to pay a prepayment penalty of as much as 1%

of the old loan balance. In addition, arranging a new loan may require payment of closing expenses, including discount points, application fee, survey fees, and title insurance. Some of these costs may be waived if the loan is with the original lender. Second mortgages have closing costs, as well. Currently, many lenders of home equity loans are reducing or waiving much of the closing costs for such loans.

Why is it important to know how much equity you have in your home?

If you want to refinance in order to take money out of your home, the amount of equity you own limits how much you can borrow. If the increased debt is more than 80% of the home's current value, you may not be able to borrow as much as you want unless you obtain mortgage insurance. If the value of your home has declined since you bought it, you may even have difficulty refinancing the loan at the same amount. Thus, you may want to have the home appraised before you apply for the loan.

What is a home equity loan?

A home equity loan essentially is a second mortgage loan that allows a homeowner to access the accumulated equity in the home. The loan may be set up as a traditional second mortgage or as a line of credit. The traditional loan provides a lump sum when the loan is closed, whereas the line of credit gives the borrower the right to draw cash over time as needed. Home equity loans became popular as real estate in many parts of the country increased in value. In addition, the federal government allows homeowners to deduct all interest payments on such loans—but not on personal debts, such as credit card interest—from their income taxes. Borrowers thus may be able to reduce their after-tax cost of credit by converting nondeductible consumer loans to mortgage loans. (See next question.)

How can I save taxes with a home equity loan?

The Tax Reform Act of 1986 phased out itemized deductions for consumer interest. However, the deductibility of mortgage interest was left intact. In addition to the original loan used to purchase the home, up to $100,000 of additional mortgage debt qualifies for interest deductions. If you have considerable consumer debt—auto loans, college loans, credit card balances—you may want to take out a home equity loan and pay off these loans. If you commonly carry a balance on your credit cards or retail credit accounts, you can get a home equity line of credit that allows access through a credit card.

I'm retired and have paid off my mortgage. My house is valuable and I need cash income, but I don't want to sell. Is there a way to increase my retirement income?

You may want to consider a home equity conversion loan. Programs allow elderly homeowners to mortgage their home in such a way that the lender will provide monthly payments of supplemental income. The amount of income depends on a number of choices. The balance of the loan is paid out of the proceeds when the home is sold.

I have a fixed-rate loan. Can I take advantage of recent reductions in interest rates?

When rates have dropped, you may take out a new loan at the lower rate and pay off the old loan. In most cases, the new loan is just enough to pay the old loan balance. However, you may want to include a little extra to cover the closing costs on the new loan. After the change, you will enjoy lower monthly payments. On the other hand, you may be able to structure the new loan to give you the same payments you currently have, but for a higher balance. The additional proceeds from the new loan could be used to pay off other debts.

How do I know when interest rates have dropped low enough to make refinancing worthwhile?

It is futile to try to guess when rates will be at their lowest level. On the other hand, there are certain guidelines to follow. For one thing, you should refinance whenever the current rate is more than one percentage point below the rate you currently have. You will want to reduce your monthly payments enough so that you can recover your refinancing costs before you move out of the home. If you calculate what your new principal and interest payment will be and compare it to your current payment (subtract out the part going to escrow), you will know your monthly savings. Dividing total refinancing costs by monthly savings indicates how many months it will take to recover costs. This assumes that savings several months from now is just as valuable as the money you have today.

The bank has offered me a discount if I pay off the balance of my loan. Should I take their offer?

The reason they are interested in retiring your loan is likely to be that your interest rate is much below the current rate. Even after giving you a discount, they can use the money to make a more valuable loan. Still, if you have the money and no other debts, and by paying off the loan you do not deplete your emergency cash, taking the offer may be the wise move. Of course, if you plan to sell the home soon, you should take their offer. You would be paying off the loan anyway as part of the sale. If you have discretionary funds, apply them first to your higher-cost debts before retiring a low-interest rate loan. Keep in mind that the discount will be considered taxable income.

What is a convertible ARM?

An ARM, or adjustable-rate mortgage, provides the lender the right to change the interest rate on the loan at specified intervals. While this means that you can reduce your payments when interest rates fall, without refinancing, you are vulnerable to increases in rates. Some ARMs have a feature that allows the borrower to convert the loan to a fixed interest rate at some point in the loan term. When interest rates decline, you may convert and lock in the rate for the remainder of the term. Conversely, some loans begin as fixed-rate, then convert to an ARM automatically after a few years.

I want to add a room to my home. How do I finance it?

You may refinance the first mortgage to provide additional funds for the work, you may add a second mortgage, or you may take out a home equity loan. Even though the improvement may add to the value of your home, the lender may insist that you have sufficient equity based on the home's current value to justify the loan. Another alternative is using nonmortgage loans, but be aware that interest on these loans will not be fully deductible from your income taxes.

GLOSSARY

Accrued interest interest that has been earned but not paid.

Acquisition loan money borrowed for the purpose of purchasing a property.

Adjustable-rate mortgage (ARM) mortgage loan that allows the interest rate to be changed at specific intervals over the life of the loan.

Amortization gradual paying off of a debt by periodic installments.

Amortization schedule table that shows the periodic payment, interest, and principal requirements, and unpaid loan balance for each period of the life of a loan.

Annual cap limit on the amount of adjustment in the interest rate on an adjustable-rate mortgage over a 12-month period.

Annual percentage rate effective rate of interest for a loan, per year, disclosure of which is required by the federal Truth-In-Lending law.

Annuity series of equal or nearly equal periodic payments or receipts.

Appraisal opinion or estimate of the value of a property.

Assumable loan mortgage loan that allows the purchaser of a home to undertake the obligation of the existing loan with no change in loan terms. This is generally true of loans without due-on-sale clauses. Most FHA and VA mortgages are assumable.

Assumption of mortgage purchase of mortgaged property whereby the buyer accepts liability for a debt that continues to exist. The seller remains liable to the lender unless the lender agrees to cancel or otherwise modify the obligation.

Automated Valuation Model (AVM) computerized method for estimating the value of a property that is often used for quick decisions on some mortgage loans.

Balloon payment final payment on a loan, when that payment is greater than the preceding installment payments and pays off the loan in full.

Bridge loan mortgage financing between the termination of one loan and the beginning of another loan.

Buy down (1) action to pay additional discount points to a lender in exchange for a reduced rate of interest on a loan; the reduced rate may apply for all or a portion of the loan term. (2) loan that has been bought down by the seller of the property for the benefit of the buyer.

Cap in adjustable-rate mortgages, a limit placed on adjustments to protect the borrower from large increases in the interest rate or the payment level.

Certificate of eligibility issued by the Veterans Administration to those who qualify for a VA loan.

Closing (1) act of transferring ownership of a property from seller to buyer in accordance with a sales contract. (2) the time when a closing takes place.

Closing costs various fees and expenses payable by the seller and buyer at the time of a real estate closing (also termed transaction or settlement costs).

Commercial bank financial institution authorized to provide a variety of financial services, including consumer and business loans (generally short-term), checking services, credit cards, and savings accounts. Certain deposits at most commercial banks are insured by the Federal Deposit Insurance Corporation. Commercial banks may be members of the Federal Reserve System.

Commitment pledge or promise; firm agreement.

Co-mortgagor person who signs a mortgage contract with another party or parties and is thereby jointly obligated to repay the loan. Generally, a co-mortgagor provides some assistance in meeting the requirements of the loan and receives a share of ownership in the encumbered property.

Conforming loan mortgage loan that fits the criteria specified by the Federal National Mortgage Association (Fannie Mae) and Federal Home Loan Mortgage Corporation (Freddie Mac) for loans they purchase. Most often, nonconforming loans are those that exceed the statutory limits on the amount of loan the agencies may purchase.

Construction loan one that finances subdivision costs and/or improvements to real estate.

Conventional loan a mortgage loan other than one guaranteed by the Veterans Administration or insured by the Federal Housing Administration.

Convertible ARM an adjustable-rate mortgage that offers the borrower the option to convert payments to a fixed-rate schedule at a specified period within the term of the loan. Conversion is made for a nominal fee, and the interest rate on the fixed-rate loan is determined by a rule specified in the ARM loan agreement.

Credit rating (report) evaluation of a person's capacity for (or history of) debt repayment. Generally available for individuals from a local retail credit association. In addition, under certain circumstances, individuals have access to their own files.

Deed of trust instrument used in many states in lieu of a mortgage. Legal title to the property is vested in one or more trustees to secure the repayment of the loan.

Default failure to fulfill an obligation or promise, or to perform specified acts.

Deficiency judgment court order stating that the borrower still owes money when the security for a loan does not entirely satisfy a defaulted debt.

Discount points amounts paid to the lender (usually by the seller) at the time of origination of a loan, to account for the difference between the market interest rate and the lower face rate of the note.

Down payment amount one pays for property in addition to the debt incurred.

Due-on-sale clause provision in a mortgage stating that the loan is due upon the sale of the property.

Effective rate true rate of return, considering all relevant financing expenses.

Entitlement for a VA loan, the dollar amount of loan guarantee that the Veterans Benefits Administration (VA) provides to each eligible veteran. VA loan guarantees are available to military veterans who served in the armed services during specified war periods. The guarantee allows the veteran to borrow money to buy a home without the need for a cash down payment. Generally, lenders will lend up to four times the amount of the entitlement with no cash investment by the borrower.

Equity interest or value that the owner has in real estate over and above the liens against it.

Escrow agreement between two or more parties providing that certain instruments or property be placed with a third party for safekeeping, pending the fulfillment or performance of a specified act or condition.

Escrow payment part of the borrower's monthly payment that goes into an account (called *escrow, impound,* or *trust*) to pay property taxes and insurance when they become due.

Exculpatory clause provision in a mortgage allowing the borrower to surrender the property to the lender without personal liability for the loan.

Familial status characteristic determined by a person's household type, such as marriage and existing or prospective children. Referred to in the Federal Fair Housing Law and Fair Credit Reporting Act; prohibits denying rights to people under 18 who live with a parent or legal guardian. Pregnant women are specifically covered.

Federal Housing Administration (FHA) agency of the U.S. government, Department of Housing and Urban Development, that administers many loan programs, loan guarantee programs, and loan insurance programs designed to make more housing available.

FICO (Fair Isaac Company) scores a measure of borrower credit risk commonly used by mortgage loan underwriters when originating loans on owner-occupied homes. The score is based on the applicants' credit history and how much they use credit. Expressed as a number between 300 and 850, the score determines not only whether the loan is approved, but also what type of terms are offered by the lender.

Finance clause or **finance addendum** attachment to an agreement of sale that states conditions for financing the property that must be met for the buyer to be held to close the sale. Examples of conditions that might be specified in such a clause or addendum are:

• minimum amount to be financed
• minimum loan-to-value ratio
• maximum interest rate
• maximum discount points
• maximum origination fees

First mortgage mortgage that has priority as a lien over all other mortgages; in cases of foreclosure, the first mortgage will be satisfied before other mortgages.

Fixed-rate mortgage loan secured by real property featuring an interest rate that is constant for the term of the loan. Contrast *Adjustable-rate mortgage.*

Foreclosure termination of all rights of a mortgagor or the grantee in the property covered by the mortgage. Statutory foreclosure is effected without recourse to courts, but must conform to laws (statutes). Strict foreclosure forever bars equity of redemption.

Full amortization term the amount of time it will take a mortgage to be fully retired through periodic payments of principal and interest.

Funding fee (VA) a nominal fee charged by the Veterans Benefits Administration to those receiving a mortgage loan guaranteed by the Administration.

Guarantee (a loan) to agree to indemnify the holder of a loan all or a portion of the unpaid principal balance in case of default by the borrower.

High-ratio mortgage/loan a loan that requires a small percentage cash down payment; generally, a loan that covers more than 80% of the value of the mortgaged property. Such loans generally require loan insurance or guarantee.

Home equity conversion mortgage (HECM) a reverse mortgage insured by the FHA.

Home equity line of credit a type of home equity loan that establishes an account that the borrower can draw upon as desired. The account generally sets an upper limit on the amount of outstanding debt, similar to a credit card. Interest accrues based on the amount of money actually borrowed, not the amount of the credit line. The product is intended for people who may need to access cash in the future, but have no immediate need for a loan.

Housing counseling agencies private, nonprofit, and government entities that provide educational, advisory, and credit counseling services to those attempting to obtain housing. Services are oriented toward lower-income clients. A training program is required to qualify for many first-time homebuyer loans.

Housing finance agency governmental (state or local) organization established to provide housing assistance. In most cases, the agency can issue bonds that pay tax-free interest and therefore sell at below-market yields. The low-cost money is then used to fund low-interest mortgage loans for eligible borrowers. The amount of bond financing available to each state is limited by the U.S. Treasury.

Hybrid mortgage one that has elements of both fixed-rate and adjustable-rate mortgages. For example, a 5/25 is a hybrid mortgage loan that requires 5 years at a low fixed interest rate, after which the interest rate rises to the market rate for the next 25 years. Also popular are the 3/27 and 7/23 hybrids.

Initial rate period the time from origination of an adjustable-rate mortgage and the expiration of the initial interest rate. The period usually extends to the date of the first allowable interest rate adjustment. After this period, the loan's interest rate is adjusted to conform with the index applied to the loan.

Insurance (mortgage) a policy, generally purchased by a borrower, that will indemnify the lender in case of fore-closure of the loan. Indemnification is generally limited to losses suffered by the lender in the foreclosure process.

Interim financing loan, including a construction loan, used when the property owner is unable or unwilling to arrange permanent financing; generally arranged for less than three years, and used to gain time for financial or market conditions to improve.

Jumbo mortgage a loan for an amount exceeding the statutory limit placed on the size of loans that Freddie Mac and Fannie Mae can purchase. Such loans must be maintained in the lender's portfolio or sold to private investors. These loans are often required for purchase of luxury homes.

Junior mortgage mortgage whose claim against the property will be satisfied only after prior mortgages have been repaid.

Junk fees charges levied by a lender at closing in the hope that the borrower will not question them nor will they abort the transaction. Such fees are often of a questionable nature, but they are small relative to other legitimate closing costs.

Lender general term applied to any party that originates or holds loans.

Leverage use of borrowed funds to increase purchasing power and, ideally, to increase the profitability of an investment.

Lien charge against property, making it security for the payment of a debt, judgment, mortgage, or taxes; it is a type of encumbrance. A *specific lien* is against certain property only. A *personal lien* is against all of the property owned by the debtor.

Life of loan cap contractual limitation on the maximum interest rate that can be applied to an adjustable-rate mortgage during the term of the loan.

Line of credit agreement whereby a financial institution promises to lend up to a certain amount without the need to file another application.

Loan application document required by a lender prior to issuing a loan commitment. The application generally includes the following information:
1. name of the borrower
2. amount and terms of the loan
3. description of the subject property to be mortgaged

Loan commitment agreement to lend money, generally of a specified amount, at specified terms at some time in the future.

Loan discount see *discount points*.

Loan lock see *locked-in interest rate*.

Loan modification adjustment of the terms of a loan during its term in a way not accounted for in the original loan contract, but accepted later by mutual consent of the lender and borrower. Usually a concession to the borrower in an attempt to avoid foreclosure.

Loan processing the steps a lender takes in the loan approval process, from application for a home mortgage through to closing.

Loan-to-value ratio (LTV) proportion of the amount borrowed compared to the cost or value of the property purchased.

Locked-in interest rate the rate promised by a lender at the time of the application. The promise is a legal commitment of the lender, though there may be qualifications or contingencies that allow the lender to charge a higher rate. On home loans, the lock-in is customarily provided for 1% of the amount borrowed, though often it is free of charge.

Margin constant amount added to the value of the index for the purpose of adjusting the interest rate on an adjustable-rate mortgage.

Maturity due date of a loan.

Mortgage written instrument that creates a lien upon real estate as security for the payment of a specified debt.

Mortgage banker one who originates, sells, and services mortgage loans. Most loans are insured or guaranteed by a government agency or private mortgage insurer.

Mortgage broker an agent who finds borrowers for one or more lenders. The broker may perform all or part of the loan application process, as well.

Mortgage constant percentage ratio between the annual debt service and the loan principal. The formula is

$$\frac{\text{Annual debt service}}{\text{Loan principal}} = \text{mortgage constant}$$

Mortgage lien encumbrance on property used to secure a loan. The holder of the lien has a claim to the property in case of loan default. The priority of the claim depends on the order of recording and any subordination agreements. Thus, the holder of a first mortgage generally has claim that runs prior to the claims of all other mortgage lien holders.

Mortgage note the document that states the names of the borrower and lender, amount borrowed, interest rate, repayment terms, and other loan provisions. The mortgage pledges property as collateral; the note provides the amount of debt and repayment requirements.

Mortgaged property real or personal property that has been pledged as security for a loan.

Mortgagee one who holds a lien on property or title to property as security for a debt.

Mortgagee's title insurance policy that protects the lender from future claims to ownership of the mortgaged property. Generally required by the lender as a condition of making a mortgage loan. In the event of a successful ownership claim from someone other than the mortgagor (borrower), the insurance company compensates the lender for any consequent loss. See *title insurance.*

Mortgagor one who pledges property as security for a loan.

Mortgagor's title insurance policy that protects the buyer/owner of real property from successful claims of ownership interest to the property. The coverage is usually supplemental to a mortgagee's title insurance policy, and the premium is customarily paid by the buyer. May also be referred to as the *owner's title policy.*

Negative amortization increase in the outstanding balance of a loan resulting from the insufficiency of payments to cover required interest charged on the loan.

Nonconforming loan loan that does not meet the standards of, or is too large to be purchased by, FNMA or FHLMC. The interest rate is at least half a percentage point higher than for a conforming loan. See *jumbo mortgage.*

Note written instrument that acknowledges a debt and states a promise to pay.

Origination fees charges to a borrower to cover the costs of issuing the loan, such as credit checks, appraisal, and title expenses.

Payoff (amount) the remaining amount of a loan, including any prepayment penalty.

Permanent mortgage mortgage for a long period of time (over 10 years).

PITI principal, interest, taxes, and insurance. Refers to the monthly payment required for most home mortgage loans. The tax and insurance portion of the payment is the monthly deposit to the escrow account used to pay property taxes and hazard insurance premiums.

Points see *discount points*.

Pre-approval the practice by a lender of approving a borrower for a certain loan amount. This allows prospective homebuyers to shop with the knowledge, likely to be shared with a seller and broker to demonstrate their financial capability, that the loan will be approved. Contrast *pre-qualification*.

Predatory lending a practice attributed to certain mortgage lenders that seeks to take advantage of the ignorance or gullibility of borrowers. Often associated with refinancing, home equity lending, or home improvement lending, these practices take on several forms: saddling borrowers with more debt than they can handle, tricking a borrower into a loan with high rates and fees, and overcharging or charging twice for required services.

Prepayment penalty fees paid by borrowers for the privilege of retiring a loan early.

Pre-qualification an informal estimate of the maximum home price a prospective buyer can arrange. Often done as a service by the real estate agent, who is concerned about focusing on houses in the appropriate price range.

Principal (1) one who owns or will use property; (2) one who contracts for the services of an agent or broker, the broker's or agent's client; (3) the amount of money raised by a mortgage or other loan, as distinct from the interest paid on it.

Principal and interest payment (P&I) periodic payment, usually paid monthly, that includes the interest charges for the period plus an amount applied to amortization of the principal balance. Commonly used with amortizing loans.

Principal residence place one lives in most of the time. May be a single-family house, condominium, cooperative apartment, trailer, or houseboat. In order to defer capital gain taxes on the profit from a home, the home must be used as the taxpayer's principal residence.

Private mortgage insurance default insurance on conventional loans provided by private insurance companies.

Purchase money mortgage mortgage given by a grantee (buyer) to a grantor (seller) in partial payment of the purchase price of real estate.

Qualifying ratio one that provides a test of lender risk exposure by limiting the amount of debt service burden a borrower is allowed to undertake. Specific ratios vary by loan product, generally being higher for loans designed for first-time buyers.

Redeem (mortgage) to cure a default by paying all overdue loan payments and penalties after receiving a notice of default, but before the lender can foreclose the mortgage.

Refinance substitute of (a) new loan(s) for (an) old loan(s).

Retire (a debt) to pay off the principal on a loan, thereby fulfilling the obligation under the loan contract.

Reverse mortgage a type of mortgage, designed for elderly home owners with substantial equity, by which a lender periodically (monthly, for example) pays an amount to the borrower. The loan balance increases with interest and periodic payments, causing negative amortization. The nonrecourse loan is paid from proceeds from future sale of the home.

Savings & loan associations (S&Ls) depository institutions that specialize in originating, servicing, and holding mortgage loans, primarily on owner-occupied, residential property.

Secondary mortgage market mechanisms available to buy and sell mortgages, mainly residential first mortgages. There is no set meeting place for the secondary mortgage market. FNMA and Freddie Mac hold auctions weekly to buy those mortgages offered at the highest effective rate. Bids are collected from all over the country.

Second home residence that is not one's principal residence. Under the Tax Reform Act of 1986, a taxpayer may deduct interest on two personal residences.

Second mortgage subordinated lien, created by a mortgage loan, over the amount of a first mortgage. Second mortgages are used at purchase to reduce the amount of a cash down payment or in refinancing to raise cash for any purpose.

Subject property in appraisal, the property being appraised.

Subject to mortgage circumstance in which a buyer takes title to mortgaged real property but is not personally liable for the payment of the amount due. The buyer must make payments in order to keep the property; however, with default, only the buyer's equity in that property is lost. Contrast *assumption of mortgage*.

Subprime refers to borrowers and loans available to borrowers with significant blemishes on their credit records. Such loans often require higher interest than standard loans.

Tax bracket marginal rate for income taxes; the percentage of each additional dollar in income required to be paid as income taxes.

Teaser rate contract interest rate charged on an adjustable-rate mortgage for the initial adjustment interval that is significantly lower than the fully indexed rate prevailing at the time. Thus, this rate is an incentive to encourage borrowers to accept adjustable-rate mortgage loans. In general, the interest rate reverts to the fully indexed rate at the first adjustment date.

Term, amortization for a loan, the period of time during which principal and interest payments must be made; generally, the time needed to amortize the loan fully.

Title insurance an insurance policy that protects the holder from loss sustained by defects in the title. Required for nearly all loans on real estate.

Transaction costs the costs associated with buying and selling a home. The following are typical costs: appraisal fees; brokerage commission (usually paid by the seller); legal fees (often including fees to the mortgagee's attorney); mortgage discount points; mortgage origination fees; recording fees; survey fees; title search.

Unsecured loan a debt that has no collateral or security.

Vacation home dwelling used by the owner occasionally for recreational or resort purposes. It may be rented to others for a portion of the year. Income tax deductions pertaining to vacation homes depend on the frequency of use by the owner. Generally, a business loss cannot be claimed on a vacation home.

VA loan home loan guaranteed by the Veterans Administration (VA) under the Servicemen's Readjustment Act of 1944 and later revisions. The VA guarantees restitution to the lender in the event of default. The guarantee is a percentage of the loan, which is changed regularly to keep up with inflation. There is also a limit. The home must be the borrower's principal residence.

USE OF CALCULATORS

If you have a financial calculator—a hand calculator that has the capability of doing compound interest using "bond buttons"—you can easily calculate payments and balances, such as those in the examples given in Key 25. To find the monthly payment on a mortgage loan, do this (the example will be worked with a HP calculator):

1. Always clear the financial registers for each new calculation.
2. Make sure the calculator is set for monthly payments.
3. Enter the term of the loan into the "*n*" button (for the example, enter 300 months and push *n*).
4. Enter the interest rate into the "*i*," "*int*," or "*I/YR*" button (enter 7 and push *I/YR*).
5. Enter the loan amount into the "*PV*" button (enter –140,000 and push *PV*).
6. The monthly payment will be printed out when you push the "*PMT*" button (yielding the result 989.49).

You also can use your financial calculator to find the cost of new money. Let's do the calculations in example 1:

1. Enter the term of the loan into the "*n*" button (enter 300 and press *n*).
2. Enter the amount of new money raised into the "*PV*" button (enter – 40,000 and press *PV*).
3. Enter the increase in the monthly payments into the "*PMT*" button (enter 345.19 and press *PMT*).
4. The rate is shown when you press the "*I/YR*" button (press *I/YR* and see the result 9.35%).

Here's how to find the loan balance in Key 26 using a financial calculator:

1. Enter the remaining term in months and press the "*n*" button (for the new first loan, enter 300 months and press *n*).
2. Enter the annual interest rate and press "*I/YR*" (enter 7 and press *I/YR*).
3. Enter the monthly payment and press "*PMT*" (enter –1297.34 and press *PMT*).
4. The remaining balance will be shown when you press "*PV*" (press *PV* and the result is 183,556.62).

The time value of money is the basis for the "bond" keys incorporated into all financial calculators (such as the HP 10B calculator commonly used by real estate professionals). Most calculators allow you to set the frequency of compounding. In most cases having to do with mortgage loans, payments are collected on a monthly basis, and the borrower is given credit for paying interest each month. Therefore, calculations should done with monthly compounding. Set the payments per year (*p/yr*) to 12 before making any calculations. Also, mortgage payments are made in arrears—at the end of the interest accruing period. On the HP calculator, the default is payment in arrears so there is no need to change it to payment in advance. Make sure that there is no message in the window saying "begin" because that erroneously computes payments at the beginning of each period. Also, either the amount you borrow in input as a negative number and the payment as a positive or vice versa; that is, the amount borrowed and the payment will have opposite signs.

There are several things you can do using the bond buttons, including finding the monthly payment, finding the loan balance at any period in the loan term, finding the cost of new money and finding how long it would take to pay off a mortgage.

Monthly Payments (An example is worked out in parentheses using HP procedures.)

1. Enter the term of the loan (in months) and press "*n*" (360 months).
2. Enter the annual interest rate in percent and press "*I/YR*" (7%).
3. Enter the amount borrowed as a negative number and press "*PV*" (–$100,000).
4. Press "*PMT*" to calculate the monthly payment amount ($665.30).

Loan Balance

1. Enter the number of payments (months) remaining in the loan term and press "*n*" (300 months).
2. Enter the annual interest rate and press "*I/YR*" (7%).
3. Enter the monthly payment as a negative number and press "*PMT*" (–$665.30).
4. Press "*PV*" to calculate the loan balance at the beginning of the remaining term ($94,131.24).

Cost of New Money (You refinance an existing loan with a larger loan to raise cash.)

1. Enter the term of the new loan in months and press "*n*" (360 months).
2. Enter the amount by which the new loan exceeds the balance of the existing loan—the cash raised by the refinancing—as a negative number and press "*PV*" (–$50,000).
3. Enter the amount by which the new monthly payment exceeds that of the existing loan and press "*PMT*" ($250).
4. Press "*I/YR*" to calculate the cost of the new money as a percentage rate (4.39%).

Term to Pay Off Loan (You make an extra payment to principal and want to know how many more months it will take to retire the loan based on your regular monthly payment.)

1. Enter the annual interest rate in percent and press "*I/YR*" (7%).
2. Enter the remaining loan balance after your extra payment is credited as a negative number and press "*PV*" (–$96,500).
3. Enter the regular monthly payment, excluding escrow and mortgage insurance, and press "*PMT*" ($687.81).
4. Press "*n*" to calculate the remaining term in months (293.3 or 24 years, 6 months with a smaller payment in the last month).

Table 1
Monthly Principal and Interest Payments
per $1,000 of Principal

Term (Years)	Contract Interest Rate (%)				
	5.00	6.00	7.00	8.00	9.00
1	$85.61	$86.07	$86.53	$86.99	$87.45
2	43.87	44.32	44.77	45.23	45.68
3	29.97	30.42	30.88	31.34	31.80
4	23.03	23.49	23.95	24.41	24.89
5	18.87	19.33	19.80	20.28	20.76
6	16.10	16.57	17.05	17.53	18.03
7	14.13	14.61	15.09	15.59	16.09
8	12.66	13.14	13.63	14.14	14.65
9	11.52	12.01	12.51	13.02	13.54
10	10.61	11.10	11.61	12.13	12.67
11	9.86	10.37	10.88	11.42	11.96
12	9.25	9.76	10.28	10.82	11.38
13	8.73	9.25	9.78	10.33	10.90
14	8.29	8.81	9.35	9.91	10.49
15	7.91	8.44	8.99	9.56	10.14
16	7.58	8.11	8.67	9.25	9.85
17	7.29	7.83	8.40	8.98	9.59
18	7.03	7.58	8.16	8.75	9.36
19	6.80	7.36	7.94	8.55	9.17
20	6.60	7.16	7.75	8.36	9.00
21	6.42	6.99	7.58	8.20	8.85
22	6.25	6.83	7.43	8.06	8.71
23	6.10	6.69	7.30	7.93	8.59
24	5.97	6.56	7.18	7.82	8.49
25	5.85	6.44	7.07	7.72	8.39
26	5.73	6.34	6.97	7.63	8.31
27	5.63	6.24	6.88	7.54	8.23
28	5.54	6.15	6.80	7.47	8.16
29	5.45	6.07	6.72	7.40	8.10
30	5.37	6.00	6.65	7.34	8.05

Table 1 (continued)
Monthly Principal and Interest Payments
per $1,000 of Principal

Term (Years)	Contract Interest Rate (%)				
	10.00	11.00	12.00	13.00	14.00
1	$87.92	$88.38	$88.85	$89.32	$89.79
2	46.14	46.61	47.07	47.54	48.01
3	32.27	32.74	33.21	33.69	34.18
4	25.36	25.85	26.33	26.83	27.33
5	21.25	21.74	22.24	22.75	23.27
6	18.53	19.03	19.55	20.07	20.61
7	16.60	17.12	17.65	18.19	18.74
8	15.17	15.71	16.25	16.81	17.37
9	14.08	14.63	15.18	15.75	16.33
10	13.22	13.78	14.35	14.93	15.53
11	12.52	13.09	13.68	14.28	14.89
12	11.95	12.54	13.13	13.75	14.37
13	11.48	12.08	12.69	13.31	13.95
14	11.08	11.69	12.31	12.95	13.60
15	10.75	11.37	12.00	12.65	13.32
16	10.46	11.09	11.74	12.40	13.08
17	10.21	10.85	11.51	12.19	12.87
18	10.00	10.65	11.32	12.00	12.70
19	9.81	10.47	11.15	11.85	12.56
20	9.65	10.32	11.01	11.72	12.44
21	9.51	10.19	10.89	11.60	12.33
22	9.38	10.07	10.78	11.50	12.24
23	9.27	9.97	10.69	11.42	12.16
24	9.17	9.88	10.60	11.34	12.10
25	9.09	9.80	10.53	11.28	12.04
26	9.01	9.73	10.47	11.22	11.99
27	8.94	9.67	10.41	11.17	11.95
28	8.88	9.61	10.37	11.13	11.91
29	8.82	9.57	10.32	11.09	11.88
30	8.78	9.52	10.29	11.06	11.85

Table 2
Monthly Mortgage Payments
6% Interest Rate

Principal Amount	Full Amortization Term (Years)			
	15	20	25	30
10,000	84.39	71.65	64.44	59.96
20,000	168.78	143.29	128.87	119.92
30,000	253.16	214.93	193.30	179.87
40,000	337.55	286.58	257.73	239.83
50,000	421.93	358.22	322.16	299.78
60,000	506.32	429.86	386.59	359.74
70,000	590.70	501.51	451.02	419.69
80,000	675.09	573.15	515.45	479.65
90,000	759.48	644.79	579.88	539.60
100,000	843.86	716.44	644.31	599.56
110,000	928.25	788.08	708.74	659.51
120,000	1,012.63	859.72	773.17	719.47
130,000	1,097.02	931.37	837.60	779.42
140,000	1,181.40	1,003.01	902.03	839.38
150,000	1,265.79	1,074.65	966.46	899.33
160,000	1,350.18	1,146.29	1,030.89	959.29
170,000	1,434.56	1,217.94	1,095.32	1,019.24
180,000	1,518.95	1,289.58	1,159.75	1,079.20
190,000	1,603.33	1,361.22	1,224.18	1,139.15
200,000	1,687.72	1,432.87	1,288.61	1,199.11
210,000	1,772.10	1,504.51	1,353.04	1,259.06
220,000	1,856.49	1,576.15	1,417.47	1,319.02
230,000	1,940.88	1,647.80	1,481.90	1,378.97
240,000	2,025.26	1,719.44	1,546.33	1,438.93
250,000	2,109.65	1,791.08	1,610.76	1,498.88
260,000	2,194.03	1,862.73	1,675.19	1,558.84
270,000	2,278.42	1,934.37	1,739.62	1,618.79
280,000	2,362.80	2,006.01	1,804.05	1,678.75
290,000	2,447.19	2,077.65	1,868.48	1,738.70
300,000	2,531.58	2,149.30	1,932.91	1,798.66
400,000	3,375.43	2,865.72	2,577.21	2,398.20
500,000	4,219.28	3,582.16	3,221.51	2,997.75
600,000	5,063.14	4,298.59	3,865.81	3,597.30
700,000	5,907.00	5,015.02	4,510.11	4,196.85
800,000	6,750.85	5,731.45	5,154.41	4,796.40
900,000	7,594.71	6,447.88	5,798.71	5,395.95
1,000,000	8,438.57	7,164.31	6,443.01	5,995.51

Table 2 (continued)
Monthly Mortgage Payments
6.25% Interest Rate

Principal	Full Amortization Term (Years)			
Amount	15	20	25	30
10,000	85.75	73.10	65.97	61.58
20,000	171.49	146.19	131.94	123.15
30,000	257.23	219.28	197.91	184.72
40,000	342.97	292.38	263.87	246.29
50,000	428.72	365.47	329.84	307.86
60,000	514.46	438.56	395.81	369.44
70,000	600.20	511.65	461.77	431.01
80,000	685.94	584.75	527.74	492.58
90,000	771.69	657.84	593.71	554.15
100,000	857.43	730.93	659.67	615.72
110,000	943.17	804.03	725.64	677.29
120,000	1,028.91	877.12	791.61	738.87
130,000	1,114.65	950.21	857.58	800.44
140,000	1,200.40	1,023.30	923.54	862.01
150,000	1,286.14	1,096.40	989.51	923.58
160,000	1,371.88	1,169.49	1,055.48	985.15
170,000	1,457.62	1,242.58	1,121.44	1,046.72
180,000	1,543.37	1,315.68	1,187.41	1,108.30
190,000	1,629.11	1,388.77	1,253.38	1,169.87
200,000	1,714.85	1,461.86	1,319.34	1,231.44
210,000	1,800.59	1,534.95	1,385.31	1,293.01
220,000	1,886.34	1,608.05	1,451.28	1,354.58
230,000	1,972.08	1,681.14	1,517.24	1,416.15
240,000	2,057.82	1,754.23	1,583.21	1,477.73
250,000	2,143.56	1,827.33	1,649.18	1,539.30
260,000	2,229.30	1,900.42	1,715.15	1,600.87
270,000	2,315.05	1,973.51	1,781.11	1,662.44
280,000	2,400.79	2,046.60	1,847.08	1,724.01
290,000	2,486.53	2,119.70	1,913.05	1,785.58
300,000	2,572.27	2,192.79	1,979.01	1,847.16
400,000	3,429.69	2,923.71	2,638.68	2,462.87
500,000	4,287.11	3,654.64	3,298.35	3,078.59
600,000	5,144.54	4,385.57	3,958.02	3,694.30
700,000	6,001.96	5,116.50	4,617.69	4,310.02
800,000	6,859.38	5,847.43	5,277.36	4,925.74
900,000	7,716.81	6,578.35	5,937.02	5,541.45
1,000,000	8,574.23	7,309.28	6,596.69	6,157.17

Table 2 (continued)
Monthly Mortgage Payments
6.50% Interest Rate

Principal	Full Amortization Term (Years)			
Amount	15	20	25	30
10,000	87.12	74.56	67.53	63.21
20,000	174.23	149.12	135.05	126.42
30,000	261.34	223.68	202.57	189.63
40,000	348.45	298.23	270.09	252.83
50,000	435.56	372.79	337.61	316.04
60,000	522.67	447.35	405.13	379.25
70,000	609.78	521.91	472.65	442.45
80,000	696.89	596.46	540.17	505.66
90,000	784.00	671.02	607.69	568.87
100,000	871.11	745.58	675.21	632.07
110,000	958.22	820.14	742.73	695.28
120,000	1,045.33	894.69	810.25	758.49
130,000	1,132.44	969.25	877.77	821.69
140,000	1,219.56	1,043.81	945.29	884.90
150,000	1,306.67	1,118.36	1,012.82	948.11
160,000	1,393.78	1,192.92	1,080.34	1,011.31
170,000	1,480.89	1,267.48	1,147.86	1,074.52
180,000	1,568.00	1,342.04	1,215.38	1,137.73
190,000	1,655.11	1,416.59	1,282.90	1,200.93
200,000	1,742.22	1,491.15	1,350.42	1,264.14
210,000	1,829.33	1,565.71	1,417.94	1,327.35
220,000	1,916.44	1,640.27	1,485.46	1,390.55
230,000	2,003.55	1,714.82	1,552.98	1,453.76
240,000	2,090.66	1,789.38	1,620.50	1,516.97
250,000	2,177.77	1,863.94	1,688.02	1,580.17
260,000	2,264.88	1,938.50	1,755.54	1,643.38
270,000	2,351.99	2,013.05	1,823.06	1,706.59
280,000	2,439.11	2,087.61	1,890.58	1,769.80
290,000	2,526.22	2,162.17	1,958.11	1,833.00
300,000	2,613.33	2,236.72	2,025.63	1,896.21
400,000	3,484.43	2,982.29	2,700.83	2,528.27
500,000	4,355.54	3,727.87	3,376.04	3,160.34
600,000	5,226.64	4,473.44	4,051.24	3,792.41
700,000	6,097.75	5,219.01	4,726.45	4,424.48
800,000	6,968.86	5,964.59	5,401.66	5,056.54
900,000	7,839.97	6,710.16	6,076.86	5,688.61
1,000,000	8,711.07	7,455.73	6,752.07	6,320.68

Table 2 (continued)
Monthly Mortgage Payments
6.75% Interest Rate

Principal	Full Amortization Term (Years)			
Amount	15	20	25	30
10,000	88.50	76.04	69.10	64.86
20,000	176.99	152.08	138.19	129.72
30,000	265.48	228.11	207.28	194.58
40,000	353.97	304.15	276.37	259.44
50,000	442.46	380.19	345.46	324.30
60,000	530.95	456.22	414.55	389.16
70,000	619.44	532.26	483.64	454.02
80,000	707.93	608.30	552.73	518.88
90,000	796.42	684.33	621.83	583.74
100,000	884.91	760.37	690.92	648.60
110,000	973.41	836.41	760.01	713.46
120,000	1,061.90	912.44	829.10	778.32
130,000	1,150.39	988.48	898.19	843.18
140,000	1,238.88	1,064.51	967.28	908.04
150,000	1,327.37	1,140.55	1,036.37	972.90
160,000	1,415.86	1,216.59	1,105.46	1,037.76
170,000	1,504.35	1,292.62	1,174-55	1,102.62
180,000	1,592.84	1,368.66	1,243-65	1,167.48
190,000	1,681.33	1,444.70	1,312.74	1,232.34
200,000	1,769.82	1,520.73	1,381.83	1,297.20
210,000	1,858.31	1,596.77	1,450.92	1,362.06
220,000	1,946.81	1,672.81	1,520.01	1,426.92
230,000	2,035.30	1,748.84	1,589.10	1,491.78
240,000	2,123.79	1,824.88	1,658.19	1,556.64
250,000	2,212.28	11900.91	1,727.28	1,621.50
260,000	2,300.77	1,976.95	1,796.37	1,686.36
270,000	2,389.26	2,052.99	1,865.47	1,751.22
280,000	2,477.75	2,129.02	1,934.56	1,816.08
290,000	2,566.24	2,205.06	2,003.65	1,880.94
300,000	2,654.73	2,281.10	2,072.74	1,945.80
400,000	3,539.64	3,041.46	2,763.65	2,594.39
500,000	4,424.55	3,801.82	3,454.56	3,242.99
600,000	5,309.46	4,562.18	4,145.47	3,891.59
700,000	6,194.37	5,322.55	4,836.38	4,540.19
800,000	7,079.28	6,082.91	5,527.29	5,188.78
900,000	7,964.19	6,843.28	6,218.20	5,837.38
1,000,000	8,849.09	7,603.64	6,909.12	6,485.98

Table 2 (continued)
Monthly Mortgage Payments
7.00% Interest Rate

Principal Amount	Full Amortization Term (Years)			
	15	20	25	30
10,000	89.89	77.53	70.68	66.54
20,000	179.77	155.06	141.36	133.07
30,000	269.65	232.59	212.04	199.60
40,000	359.54	310.12	282.72	266.13
50,000	449.42	387.65	353.39	332.66
60,000	539.30	465.18	424.07	399.19
70,000	629.18	542.71	494.75	465.72
80,000	719.07	620.24	565.43	532.25
90,000	808.95	697.77	636.11	598.78
100,000	898.83	775.30	706.78	665.31
110,000	988.72	852.83	777.46	731.84
120,000	1,078.60	930.36	848.14	798.37
130,000	1,168.48	1,007.89	918.82	864.90
140,000	1,258.36	1,085.42	989.50	931.43
150,000	1,348.25	1,162.95	1,060.17	997.96
160,000	1,438.13	1,240.48	1,130.85	1,064.49
170,000	1,528.01	1,318.01	1,201.53	1,131.02
180,000	1,617.90	1,395.54	1,272.21	1,197.55
190,000	1,707.78	1,473.07	1,342.89	1,264.08
200,000	1,797.66	1,550.60	1,413.56	1,330.61
210,000	1,887.54	1,628.13	1,484.24	1,397.14
220,000	1,977.43	1,705.66	1,554.92	1,463.67
230,000	2,067.31	1,783.19	1,625.60	1,530.20
240,000	2,157.19	1,860.72	1,696.27	1,596.73
250,000	2,247.08	1,938.25	1,766.95	1,663.26
260,000	2,336.96	2,015.78	1,837.63	1,729.79
270,000	2,426.84	2,093.31	1,908.31	1,796.32
280,000	2,516.72	2,170.84	1,978.99	1,862.85
290,000	2,606.61	2,248.37	2,049.66	1,929.38
300,000	2,696.49	2,325.90	2,120.34	1,995.91
400,000	3,595.31	3,101.20	2,827.12	2,661.21
500,000	4,494.14	3,876.49	3,533.90	3,326.51
600,000	5,392.97	4,651.79	4,240.68	3,991.81
700,000	6,291.80	5,427.09	4,947.45	4,657.12
800,000	7,190.63	6,202.39	5,654.23	5,322.42
900,000	8,089.45	6,977.69	6,361.01	5,987.72
1,000,000	8,988.28	7,752.99	7,067.79	6,653.02

Table 2 (continued)
Monthly Mortgage Payments
7.25% Interest Rate

Principal Amount	Full Amortization Term (Years)			
	15	20	25	30
10,000	91.29	79.04	72.29	68.22
20,000	182.58	158.08	144.57	136.44
30,000	273.86	237.12	216.85	204.66
40,000	365.15	316.16	289.13	272.88
50,000	456.44	395.19	361.41	341.09
60,000	547.72	474.23	433.69	409.31
70,000	639.01	553.27	505.97	477.53
80,000	730.30	632.31	578.25	545.75
90,000	821.58	711.34	650.53	613.96
100,000	912.87	790.38	722.81	682.18
110,000	1,004.15	869.42	795.09	750.40
120,000	1,095.44	948.46	867.37	818.62
130,000	1,186.73	1,027.49	939.65	886.83
140,000	1,278.01	1,106.53	1,011.93	955.05
150,000	1,369.30	1,185.57	1,084.22	1,023.27
160,000	1,460.59	1,264.61	1,156.50	1,091.49
170,000	1,551.87	1,343.64	1,228.78	1,159.70
180,000	1,643.16	1,422.68	1,301.06	1,227.92
190,000	1,734.44	1,501.72	1,373.34	1,296.14
200,000	1,825.73	1,580.76	1,445.62	1,364.36
210,000	1,917.02	1,659.79	1,517.90	1,432.58
220,000	2,008.30	1,738.83	1,590.18	1,500.79
230,000	2,099.59	1,817.87	1,662.46	1,569.01
240,000	2,190.88	1,896.91	1,734.74	1,637.23
250,000	2,282.16	1,975.94	1,807.02	1,705.45
260,000	2,373.45	2,054.98	1,879.30	1,773.66
270,000	2,464.73	2,134.02	1,951.58	1,841.88
280,000	2,556.02	2,213.06	2,023.86	1,910.10
290,000	2,647.31	2,292.10	2,096.14	1,978.32
300,000	2,738.59	2,371.13	2,168.43	2,046.53
400,000	3,651.45	3,161.50	2,891.23	2,728.71
500,000	4,564.31	3,951.88	3,614.03	3,410.88
600,000	5,477.18	4,742.26	4,336.84	4,093.06
700,000	6,390.04	5,532.63	5,059.65	4,775.23
800,000	7,302.90	6,323.01	5,782.45	5,457.41
900,000	8,215.77	7,113.38	6,505.26	6,139.59
1,000,000	9,128.63	7,903.76	7,228.07	6,821.76

Table 2 (continued)
Monthly Mortgage Payments
7.50% Interest Rate

Principal Amount	Full Amortization Term (Years)			
	15	20	25	30
10,000	92.71	80.56	73.90	69.93
20,000	185.41	161.12	147.80	139.85
30,000	278.11	241.68	221.70	209.77
40,000	370.81	322.24	295.60	279.69
50,000	463.51	402.80	369.50	349.61
60,000	556.21	483.36	443.40	419.53
70,000	648.91	563.92	517.30	489.46
80,000	741.61	644.48	591.20	559.38
90,000	834.32	725.04	665.10	629.30
100,000	927.02	805.60	739.00	699.22
110,000	1,019.72	886.16	812.90	769.14
120,000	1,112.42	966.72	886.79	839.06
130,000	1,205.12	1,047.28	960.69	908.98
140,000	1,297.82	1,127.84	1,034.59	978.91
150,000	1,390.52	1,208.39	1,108.49	1,048.83
160,000	1,483.22	1,288.95	1,182.39	1,118.75
170,000	1,575.93	1,369.51	1,256.29	1,188.67
180,000	1,668.63	1,450.07	1,330.19	1,258.59
190,000	1,761.33	1,530.63	1,404.09	1,328.51
200,000	1,854.03	1,611.19	1,477.99	1,398.43
210,000	1,946.73	1,691.75	1,551.89	1,468.36
220,000	2,039.43	1,772.31	1,625.79	1,538.28
230,000	2,132.13	1,852.87	1,699.68	1,608.20
240,000	2,224.83	1,933.43	1,773.58	1,678.12
250,000	2,317.54	2,013.99	1,847.48	1,748.04
260,000	2,410.24	2,094.55	1,921.38	1,817.96
270,000	2,502.94	2,175.11	1,995.28	1,887.88
280,000	2,595.64	2,255.67	2,069.18	1,957.81
290,000	2,688.34	2,336.23	2,143.08	2,027.73
300,000	2,781.04	2,416.78	2,216.98	2,097.65
400,000	3,708.05	3,222.37	2,955.96	2,796.86
500,000	4,635.06	4,027.97	3,694.96	3,496.07
600,000	5,562.07	4,833.56	4,433.95	4,195.29
700,000	6,489.09	5,639.15	5,172.94	4,894.50
800,000	7,416.10	6,444.75	5,911.93	5,593.72
900,000	8,343.11	7,250.34	6,650.92	6,292.93
1,000,000	9,270.12	8,055.93	7,389.91	6,992.15

188

Table 2 (continued)
Monthly Mortgage Payments
7.75% Interest Rate

Principal Amount	Full Amortization Term (Years)			
	15	20	25	30
10,000	94.13	82.10	75.54	71.65
20,000	188.26	164.19	151.07	143.29
30,000	282.39	246.29	226.60	214.93
40,000	376.52	328.38	302.14	286.57
50,000	470.64	410.48	377.67	358.21
60,000	564.77	492.57	453.20	429.85
70,000	658.90	574.67	528.74	501.49
80,000	753.03	656.76	604.27	573.13
90,000	847.15	738.86	679.80	644.78
100,000	941.28	820.95	755.33	716.42
110,000	1,035.41	903.05	830.87	788.06
120,000	1,129.54	985.14	906.40	859.70
130,000	1,223.66	1,067.24	981.93	931.34
140,000	1,317.79	1,149.33	1,057.47	1,002.98
150,000	1,411.92	1,231.43	1,133.00	1,074.62
160,000	1,506.05	1,313.52	1,208.53	1,146.26
170,000	1,600.17	1,395.62	1,284.06	1,217.91
180,000	1,694.30	1,477.71	1,359.60	1,289.55
190,000	1,788.43	1,559.81	1,435.13	1,361.19
200,000	1,882.56	1,641.90	1,510.66	1,432.83
210,000	1,976.68	1,724.00	1,586.20	1,504.47
220,000	2,070.81	1,806.09	1,661.73	1,576.11
230,000	2,164.94	1,888.19	1,737.26	1,647.75
240,000	2,259.07	1,970.28	1,812.79	1,719.39
250,000	2,353.19	2,052.38	1,888.33	1,791.04
260,000	2,447.32	2,134.47	1,963.86	1,862.68
270,000	2,541.45	2,216.57	2,039.39	1,934.32
280,000	2,635.58	2,298.66	2,114.93	2,005.96
290,000	2,729.70	2,380.76	2,190.46	2,077.60
300,000	2,823.83	2,462.85	2,265.99	2,149.24
400,000	3,765.10	3,283.79	3,021.32	2,865.65
500,000	4,706.38	4,104.74	3,776.64	3,582.06
600,000	5,647.65	4,925.69	4,531.97	4,298.47
700,000	6,588.93	5,746.64	5,287.30	5,014.89
800,000	7,530.21	6,567.59	6,042.63	5,731.30
900,000	8,471.48	7,388.54	6,797.96	6,447.71
1,000,000	9,412.76	8,209.49	7,553.29	7,164.12

Table 2 (continued)
Monthly Mortgage Payments
8.00% Interest Rate

Principal	Full Amortization Term (Years)			
Amount	15	20	25	30
10,000	95.57	83.65	77.19	73.38
20,000	191.14	167.29	154.37	146.76
30,000	286.70	250.94	231.55	220.13
40,000	382.27	334.58	308.73	293.51
50,000	477.83	418.22	385.91	366.89
60,000	573.40	501.87	463.09	440.26
70,000	668.96	585.51	540.28	513.64
80,000	764.53	669.16	617.46	587.02
90,000	860.09	752.80	694.64	660.39
100,000	955.66	836.44	771.82	733.77
110,000	1,051.22	920.09	849.00	807.15
120,000	1,146.79	1,003.73	926.18	880.52
130,000	1,242.35	1,087.38	1,003.37	953.90
140,000	1,337.92	1,171.02	1,080.55	1,027.28
150,000	1,433.48	1,254.67	1,157.73	1,100.65
160,000	1,529.05	1,338.31	1,234.91	1,174.03
170,000	1,624.61	1,421.95	1,312.09	1,247.40
180,000	1,720.18	1,505.60	1,389.27	1,320.78
190,000	1,815.74	1,589.24	1,466.46	1,394.16
200,000	1,911.31	1,672.89	1,543.64	1,467.53
210,000	2,006.87	1,756.53	1,620.82	1,540.91
220,000	2,102.44	1,840.17	1,698.00	1,614.29
230,000	2,198.00	1,923.82	1,775.18	1,687.66
240,000	2,293.57	2,007.46	1,852.36	1,761.04
250,000	2,389.14	2,091.11	1,929.55	1,834.42
260,000	2,484.70	2,174.75	2,006.73	1,907.79
270,000	2,580.27	2,258.39	2,083.91	1,981.17
280,000	2,675.83	2,342.04	2,161.09	2,054.55
290,000	2,771.40	2,425.68	2,238.27	2,127.92
300,000	2,866.96	2,509.33	2,315.45	2,201.30
400,000	3,822.61	3,345.76	3,087.26	2,935.06
500,000	4,778.26	4,182.20	3,859.08	3,668.82
600,000	5,733.91	5,018.64	4,630.90	4,402.59
700,000	6,689.56	5,855.08	5,402.71	5,136.35
800,000	7,645.22	6,691.52	6,174.53	5,870.12
900,000	8,600.87	7,527.96	6,946.35	6,603.88
1,000,000	9,556.52	8,364.40	7,718.16	7,337.65

Table 2 (continued)
Monthly Mortgage Payments
8.25% Interest Rate

Principal	Full Amortization Term (Years)			
Amount	15	20	25	30
10,000	97.02	85.21	78.85	75.13
20,000	194.03	170.42	157.69	150.26
30,000	291.05	255.62	236.54	225.38
40,000	388.06	340.83	315.38	300.51
50,000	485.08	426.04	394.23	375.64
60,000	582.09	511.24	473.07	450.76
70,000	679.10	596.45	551.92	525.89
80,000	776.12	681.66	630.77	601.02
90,000	873.13	766.86	709.61	676.14
100,000	970.15	852.07	788.46	751.27
110,000	1,067.16	937.28	867.30	826.40
120,000	1,164.17	1,022.48	946.15	901.52
130,000	1,261.19	1,107.69	1,024.99	976.65
140,000	1,358.20	1,192.90	1,103.84	1,051.78
150,000	1,455.22	1,278.10	1,182.68	1,126.90
160,000	1,552.23	1,363.31	1,261.53	1,202.03
170,000	1,649.24	1,448.52	1,340.37	1,277.16
180,000	1,746.26	1,533.72	1,419.22	1,352.28
190,000	1,843.27	1,618.93	1,498.06	1,427.41
200,000	1,940.29	1,704.14	1,576.91	1,502.54
210,000	2,037.30	1,789.34	1,655.75	1,577.66
220,000	2,134.31	1,874.55	1,734.60	1,652.79
230,000	2,231.33	1,959.76	1,813.44	1,727.92
240,000	2,328.34	2,044.96	1,892.29	1,803.04
250,000	2,425.36	2,130.17	1,971.13	1,878.17
260,000	2,522.37	2,215.38	2,049.98	1,953.30
270,000	2,619.38	2,300.58	2,128.82	2,028.42
280,000	2,716.40	2,385.79	2,207.67	2,103.55
290,000	2,813.41	2,471.00	2,286.51	2,178.68
300,000	2,910.43	2,556.20	2,365.36	2,253.80
400,000	3,880.56	3,408.26	3,153.80	3,005.07
500,000	4,850.70	4,260.33	3,942.25	3,756.33
600,000	5,820.84	5,112.39	4,730.70	4,507.60
700,000	6,790.98	5,964.46	5,519.15	5,258.87
800,000	7,761.12	6,816.53	6,307.60	6,010.13
900,000	8,731.26	7,668.59	7,096.05	6,761.40
1,000,000	9,701.40	8,520.66	7,884.50	7,512.67

Table 2 (continued)
Monthly Mortgage Payments
8.50% Interest Rate

Principal Amount	Full Amortization Term (Years)			
	15	20	25	30
10,000	98.48	86.79	80.53	76.90
20,000	196.95	173.57	161.05	153.79
30,000	295.43	260.35	241.57	230.68
40,000	393.90	347.13	322.10	307.57
50,000	492.37	433.92	402.62	384.46
60,000	590.85	520.70	483.14	461.35
70,000	689.32	607.48	563.66	538.24
80,000	787.80	694.26	644.19	615.14
90,000	886.27	781.05	724.71	692.03
100,000	984.74	867.83	805.23	768.92
110,000	1,083.22	954.61	885.75	845.81
120,000	1,181.69	1,041.39	966.28	922.70
130,000	1,280.17	1,128.18	1,046.80	999.59
140,000	1,378.64	1,214.96	1,127.32	1,076.48
150,000	1,477.11	1,301.74	1,207.85	1,153.38
160,000	1,575.59	1,388.52	1,288.37	1,230.27
170,000	1,674.06	1,475.30	1,368.89	1,307.16
180,000	1,772.54	1,562.09	1,449.41	1,384.05
190,000	1,871.01	1,648.87	1,529.94	1,460.94
200,000	1,969.48	1,735.65	1,610.46	1,537.83
210,000	2,067.96	1,822.43	1,690.98	1,614.72
220,000	2,166.43	1,909.22	1,771.50	1,691.61
230,000	2,264.91	1,996.00	1,852.03	1,768.51
240,000	2,363.38	2,082.78	1,932.55	1,845.40
250,000	2,461.85	2,169.56	2,013.07	1,922.29
260,000	2,560.33	2,256.35	2,093.60	1,999.18
270,000	2,658.80	2,343.13	2,174.12	2,076.07
280,000	2,757.28	2,429.91	2,254.64	2,152.96
290,000	2,855.75	2,516.69	2,335.16	2,229.85
300,000	2,954.22	2,603.47	2,415.69	2,306.75
400,000	3,938.96	3,471.29	3,220.91	3,075.65
500,000	4,923.70	4,339.12	4,026.14	3,844.57
600,000	5,908.44	5,206.94	4,831.36	4,613.48
700,000	6,893.18	6,074.76	5,636.59	5,382.39
800,000	7,877.92	6,942.59	6,441.82	6,151.31
900,000	8,862.66	7,810.41	7,247.04	6,920.22
1,000,000	9,847.40	8,678.23	8,052.27	7,689.13

Table 2 (continued)
Monthly Mortgage Payments
8.75% Interest Rate

Principal Amount	Full Amortization Term (Years)			
	15	20	25	30
10,000	99.95	88.38	82.22	78.67
20,000	199.89	176.75	164.43	157.34
30,000	299.84	265.12	246.65	236.02
40,000	399.78	353.49	328.86	314.69
50,000	499.73	441.86	411.08	393.36
60,000	599.67	530.23	493.29	472.03
70,000	699.62	618.60	575.51	550.70
80,000	799.56	706.97	657.72	629.37
90,000	899.51	795.34	739.93	708.04
100,000	999.45	883.72	822.15	786.71
110,000	1,099.40	972.09	904.36	865.38
120,000	1,199.34	1,060.46	986.58	944.05
130,000	1,299.29	1,148.83	1,068.79	1,022.72
140,000	1,399.23	1,237.20	1,151.01	1,101.39
150,000	1,499.18	1,325.57	1,233.22	1,180.06
160,000	1,599.12	1,413.94	1,315.43	1,258.73
170,000	1,699.07	1,502.31	1,397.65	1,337.40
180,000	1,799.01	1,590.68	1,479.86	1,416.07
190,000	1,898.96	1,679.06	1,562.08	1,494.74
200,000	1,998.90	1,767.43	1,644.29	1,573.41
210,000	2,098.85	1,855.80	1,726.51	1,652.08
220,000	2,198.79	1,944.17	1,808.72	1,730.75
230,000	2,298.74	2,032.54	1,890.94	1,809.42
240,000	2,398.68	2,120.91	1,973.15	1,888.09
250,000	2,498.63	2,209.28	2,055.36	1,966.76
260,000	2,598.57	2,297.65	2,137.58	2,045.43
270,000	2,698.52	2,386.02	2,219.79	2,124.10
280,000	2,798.46	2,474.39	2,302.01	2,202.77
290,000	2,898.41	2,562.77	2,384.22	2,281.44
300,000	2,998.35	2,651.14	2,466.44	2,360.11
400,000	3,997.79	3,534.84	3,288.57	3,146.80
500,000	4,997.24	4,418.55	4,110.72	3,933.50
600,000	5,996.69	5,302.26	4,932.86	4,720.20
700,000	6,996.14	6,185.97	5,755.01	5,506.90
800,000	7,995.59	7,069.69	6,577.15	6,293.60
900,000	8,995.04	7,953.40	7,399.29	7,080.30
1,000,000	9,994.49	8,837.11	8,221.44	7,867.00

Table 2 (continued)
Monthly Mortgage Payments
9.00% Interest Rate

Principal	Full Amortization Term (Years)			
Amount	15	20	25	30
10,000	101.43	89.98	83.92	80.47
20,000	202.86	179.95	167.84	160.93
30,000	304.28	269.92	251.76	241.39
40,000	405.71	359.90	335.68	321.85
50,000	507.14	449.87	419.60	402.32
60,000	608.56	539.84	503.52	482.78
70,000	709.99	629.81	587.44	563.24
80,000	811.42	719.79	671.36	643.70
90,000	912.84	809.76	755.28	724.17
100,000	1,014.27	899.73	839.20	804.63
110,000	1,115.70	989.70	923.12	885.09
120,000	1,217.12	1,079.68	1,007.04	965.55
130,000	1,318.55	1,169.65	1,090.96	1,046.01
140,000	1,419.98	1,259.62	1,174.88	1,126.48
150,000	1,521.40	1,349.59	1,258.80	1,206.94
160,000	1,622.83	1,439.57	1,342.72	1,287.40
170,000	1,724.26	1,529.54	1,426.64	1,367.86
180,000	1,825.68	1,619.51	1,510.56	1,448.33
190,000	1,927.11	1,709.48	1,594.48	1,528.79
200,000	2,028.54	1,799.46	1,678.40	1,609.25
210,000	2,129.96	1,889.43	1,762.32	1,689.71
220,000	2,231.39	1,979.40	1,846.24	1,770.17
230,000	2,332.82	2,069.37	1,930.16	1,850.64
240,000	2,434.24	2,159.35	2,014.08	1,931.10
250,000	2,535.67	2,249.32	2,098.00	2,011.56
260,000	2,637.10	2,339.29	2,181.92	2,092.02
270,000	2,738.52	2,429.26	2,265.84	2,172.49
280,000	2,839.95	2,519.24	2,349.75	2,252.95
290,000	2,941.38	2,609.21	2,433.67	2,333.41
300,000	3,042.80	2,699.18	2,517.59	2,413.87
400,000	4,057.07	3,598.90	3,356.79	3,218.49
500,000	5,071.33	4,498.63	4,195.98	4,023.11
600,000	6,085.60	5,398.36	5,035.18	4,827.74
700,000	7,099.87	6,298.08	5,874.37	5,632.36
800,000	8,114.13	7,197.81	6,713.57	6,436.98
900,000	9,128.40	8,097.53	7,552.77	7,241.60
1,000,000	10,142.67	8,997.26	8,391.96	8,046.23

Table 2 (continued)
Monthly Mortgage Payments
9.25% Interest Rate

Principal Amount	Full Amortization Term (Years)			
	15	20	25	30
10,000	102.92	91.59	85.64	82.27
20,000	205.84	183.18	171.28	164.54
30,000	308.76	274.76	256.92	246.81
40,000	411.68	366.35	342.56	329.08
50,000	514.60	457.94	428.20	411.34
60,000	617.52	549.53	513.83	493.61
70,000	720.44	641.11	599.47	575.88
80,000	823.36	732.70	685.11	658.15
90,000	926.28	824.29	770.75	740.41
100,000	1,029.20	915.87	856.39	822.68
110,000	1,132.12	1,007.46	942.02	904.95
120,000	1,235.04	1,099.05	1,027.66	987.22
130,000	1,337.95	1,190.63	1,113.30	1,069.48
140,000	1,440.87	1,282.22	1,198.94	1,151.75
150,000	1,543.79	1,373.81	1,284.58	1,234.02
160,000	1,646.71	1,465.39	1,370.22	1,316.29
170,000	1,749.63	1,556.98	1,455.85	1,398.55
180,000	1,852.55	1,648.57	1,541.49	1,480.82
190,000	1,955.47	1,740.15	1,627.13	1,563.09
200,000	2,058.39	1,831.74	1,712.77	1,645.36
210,000	2,161.31	1,923.33	1,798.41	1,727.62
220,000	2,264.23	2,014.91	1,884.04	1,809.89
230,000	2,367.15	2,106.50	1,969.68	1,892.16
240,000	2,470.07	2,198.09	2,055.32	1,974.43
250,000	2,572.99	2,289.67	2,140.96	2,056.69
260,000	2,675.90	2,381.26	2,226.60	2,138.96
270,000	2,778.82	2,472.85	2,312.24	2,221.23
280,000	2,881.74	2,564.43	2,397.87	2,303.50
290,000	2,984.66	2,656.02	2,483.51	2,385.76
300,000	3,087.58	2,747.61	2,569.15	2,468.03
400,000	4,116.77	3,663.47	3,425.53	3,290.70
500,000	5,145.96	4,579.33	4,281.91	4,113.38
600,000	6,175.15	5,495.20	5,138.29	4,936.05
700,000	7,204.35	6,411.07	5,994.67	5,758.73
800,000	8,233.54	7,326.93	6,851.05	6,581.40
900,000	9,262.73	8,242.80	7,707.44	7,404.08
1,000,000	10,291.92	9,158.67	8,563.82	8,226.75

Table 2 (continued)
Monthly Mortgage Payments
9.50% Interest Rate

Principal Amount	Full Amortization Term (Years)			
	15	**20**	**25**	**30**
10,000	104.43	93.22	87.37	84.09
20,000	208.85	186.43	174.74	168.18
30,000	313.27	279.64	262.11	252.26
40,000	417.69	372.86	349A8	336.35
50,000	522.12	466.07	436.85	420.43
60,000	626.54	559.28	524.22	504.52
70,000	730.96	652.50	611.59	588.60
80,000	835.38	745.71	698.96	672.69
90,000	939.81	838.92	786.33	756.77
100,000	1,044.23	932.14	873.70	840.86
110,000	1,148.65	1,025.35	961.07	924.94
120,000	1,253.07	1,118.56	1,048.44	1,009.03
130,000	1,357.50	1,211.78	1,135.81	1,093.12
140,000	1,461.92	1,304.99	1,223.18	1,177.20
150,000	1,566.34	1,398.20	1,310.55	1,261.29
160,000	1,670.76	1,491.41	1,397.92	1,345.37
170,000	1,775.19	1,584.63	1,485.29	1,429.46
180,000	1,879.61	1,677.84	1,572.66	1,513.54
190,000	1,984.03	1,771.05	1,660.03	1,597.63
200,000	2,088.45	1,864.27	1,747.40	1,681.71
210,000	2,192.88	1,957.48	1,834.77	1,765.80
220,000	2,297.30	2,050.69	1,922.14	1,849.88
230,000	2,401.72	2,143.91	2,009.51	1,933.97
240,000	2,506.14	2,237.12	2,096.88	2,018.05
250,000	2,610.57	2,330.33	2,184.25	2,102.14
260,000	2,714.99	2,423.55	2,271.62	2,186.23
270,000	2,819.41	2,516.76	2,358.99	2,270.31
280,000	2,923.83	2,609.97	2,446.36	2,354.40
290,000	3,028.26	2,703.19	2,533.73	2,438.48
300,000	3,132.68	2,796.40	2,621.09	2,522.57
400,000	4,176.90	3,728.52	3,494.79	3,363.42
500,000	5,221.12	4,660.66	4,368.48	4,204.27
600,000	6,265.35	5,592.79	5,242.18	5,045.13
700,000	7,309.57	6,524.92	6,115.88	5,885.98
800,000	8,353.80	7,457.05	6,989.57	6,726.83
900,000	9,398.02	8,389.18	7,863.27	7,567.69
1,000,000	10,442.25	9,321.31	8,736.97	8,408.54

Table 2 (continued)
Monthly Mortgage Payments
9.75% Interest Rate

Principal Amount	Full Amortization Term (Years)			
	15	20	25	30
10,000	105.94	94.86	89.12	85.92
20,000	211.88	189.71	178.23	171.84
30,000	317.81	284.56	267.35	257.75
40,000	423.75	379.41	356.46	343.67
50,000	529.69	474.26	445.57	429.58
60,000	635.62	569.12	534.69	515.50
70,000	741.56	663.97	623.80	601.41
80,000	847.50	758.82	712.91	687.33
90,000	953.43	853.67	802.03	773.24
100,000	1,059.37	948.52	891.14	859.16
110,000	1,165.30	1,043.37	980.26	945.07
120,000	1,271.24	1,138.23	1,069.37	1,030.99
130,000	1,377.18	1,233.08	1,158.48	1,116.91
140,000	1,483.11	1,327.93	1,247.60	1,202.82
150,000	1,589.05	1,422.78	1,336.71	1,288.74
160,000	1,694.99	1,517.63	1,425.82	1,374.65
170,000	1,800.92	1,612.48	1,514.94	1,460.57
180,000	1,906.86	1,707.34	1,604.05	1,546.48
190,000	2,012.79	1,802.19	1,693.17	1,632.40
200,000	2,118.73	1,897.04	1,782.28	1,718.31
210,000	2,224.67	1,991.89	1,871.39	1,804.23
220,000	2,330.60	2,086.74	1,960.51	1,890.14
230,000	2,436.54	2,181.59	2,049.62	1,976.06
240,000	2,542.48	2,276.45	2,138.73	2,061.98
250,000	2,648.41	2,371.30	2,227.85	2,147.89
260,000	2,754.35	2,466.15	2,316.96	2,233.81
270,000	2,860.28	2,561.00	2,406.08	2,319.72
280,000	2,966.22	2,655.85	2,495.19	2,405.64
290,000	3,072.16	2,750.70	2,584.30	2,491.55
300,000	3,178.09	2,845.56	2,673.42	2,577.47
400,000	4,237.45	3,794.07	3,564.55	3,436.62
500,000	5,296.81	4,742.58	4,455.69	4,295.77
600,000	6,356.18	5,691.10	5,346.82	5,154.93
700,000	7,415.54	6,639.62	6,237.96	6,014.08
800,000	8,474.90	7,588.13	7,129.10	6,873.24
900,000	9,534.26	8,536.65	8,020.24	7,732.39
1,000,000	10,593.63	9,485.17	8,911.37	8,591.54

Table 2 (continued)
Monthly Mortgage Payments
10.00% Interest Rate

Principal Amount	Full Amortization Term (Years)			
	15	20	25	30
10,000	107.47	96.51	90.87	87.76
20,000	214.93	193.01	181.75	175.52
30,000	322.39	289.51	272.62	263.28
40,000	429.85	386.01	363.49	351.03
50,000	537.31	482.52	454.36	438.79
60,000	644.77	579.02	545.23	526.55
70,000	752.23	675.52	636.10	614.30
80,000	859.69	772.02	726.97	702.06
90,000	967.15	868.52	817.84	789.82
100,000	1,074.61	965.03	908.71	877.58
110,000	1,182.07	1,061.53	999.58	965.33
120,000	1,289.53	1,158.03	1,090.45	1,053.09
130,000	1,396.99	1,254.53	1,181.32	1,140.85
140,000	1,504.45	1,351.04	1,272.19	1,228.61
150,000	1,611.91	1,447.54	1,363.06	1,316.36
160,000	1,719.37	1,544.04	1,453.93	1,404.12
170,000	1,826.83	1,640.54	1,544.80	1,491.88
180,000	1,934.29	1,737.04	1,635.67	1,579.63
190,000	2,041.75	1,833.55	1,726.54	1,667.39
200,000	2,149.22	1,930.05	1,817.41	1,755.15
210,000	2,256.68	2,026.55	1,908.28	1,842.91
220,000	2,364.14	2,123.05	1,999.15	1,930.66
230,000	2,471.60	2,219.55	2,090.02	2,018.42
240,000	2,579.06	2,316.06	2,180.89	2,106.18
250,000	2,686.52	2,412.56	2,271.76	2,193.93
260,000	2,793.98	2,509.06	2,362.63	2,281.69
270,000	2,901.44	2,605.56	2,453.50	2,369.45
280,000	3,008.90	2,702.07	2,544.37	2,457.21
290,000	3,116.36	2,798.57	2,635.24	2,544.96
300,000	3,223.82	2,895.07	2,726.11	2,632.72
400,000	4,298.42	3,860.09	3,634.80	3,510.29
500,000	5,373.03	4,825.11	4,543.50	4,387.86
600,000	6,447.63	5,790.13	5,452.20	5,265.43
700,000	7,522.24	6,755.15	6,360.91	6,143.00
800,000	8,596.84	7,720.17	7,269.61	7,020.57
900,000	9,671.45	8,685.19	8,178.31	7,898.14
1,000,000	10,746.05	9,650.22	9,087.01	8,775.72

INDEX